HAPPY MONEY, HAPPY FAMILY, HAPPY LEGACY

Published by Best Seller Publishing®, St. Augustine, FL
Best Seller Publishing® is a registered trademark.
Printed in the United States of America.

ISBN: 978-1-966395-11-9

For more information, please write:
Best Seller Publishing®
1775 US-1 #1070
St. Augustine, FL 32084
or call 1 (626) 765-9750

Visit us online at: www.BestSellerPublishing.org

HAPPY MONEY, HAPPY FAMILY, HAPPY LEGACY

HOW TO USE MONEY AS A TOOL TO CREATE HAPPINESS IN YOUR FAMILY'S LIFE

BY GINO BARBARO

CONTENTS

CULTIVATING A LEGACY OF HAPPINESS

This book was written more for myself than for you, the reader. That may sound like a selfish comment, but please give me the opportunity to explain. For much of my life, I've had a tumultuous relationship with money, as do many of us living in this world today, but I never really stopped to evaluate that relationship. I never took the time to reflect on why I was building an empire of real estate and what my next goals were in life.

Have you ever heard of *learn, do, and teach*? We become much better teachers when we go back and spend time learning, then implementing what we've learned. Writing this book has forced me to become a student again and has allowed me to focus on the top passions in my life: Family, Faith, and Finances.

Before this, I rarely wrote about the struggles and accomplishments that I've had as a father, raising six children and trying to teach them how to create a healthy relationship with money. My focus was always on teaching people to invest in real estate while avoiding the topics of family and fatherhood. As I put pen to paper with this book, though, I realized how important and interconnected it is to share my experiences as a parent with others and to reflect back on what has worked for me. Doing so will help me continue to focus on those aspects of parenting and become an even better father and, hopefully, grandfather someday. The similarities between raising a family and running a business became even more apparent to me as I was writing the book.

For a long time, my focus, when it came to my legacy, was always on leaving my children in a better spot than I'd been—the financial aspect of my legacy. But I was missing a much bigger and more important component: the family legacy, the legacy of what I've learned, and the values I want to pass along to future generations. How could I raise responsible children, ones who would not inherit an attitude of entitlement but instead would become stewards for the next generation? How could I prepare my children for the road ahead, rather than only prepare the road for my children?

This book made me reflect upon where I've been and where I want to lead my family into the future. My hope is that it will give you the tools and framework to lead you and your family as well.

In the first part of the book, the focus is on money. What's your relationship with money? What have you heard and been taught as a child about money? I explore the concepts of using money as a tool for happiness and understanding the definition of happy money in order to reframe how you view money—thereby teaching you and your family to become not only more financially savvy but stewards as well.

In the second part of the book, the focus is on fostering a happy family. The story continues by emphasizing the importance of being open and honest with your family and the kinds of discussions you need to be having with them every day. The focus is not only on the financial conversations but also the conversations that you, as a parent, must have and the steps you can take to continue to strengthen your family bonds.

The third section is all about crafting a happy legacy. Before writing the book, my goals with my legacy were primarily financial. However, once I sat down and explored what I wanted my legacy to look like, I found that what I truly wanted to pass down were my values, my love for my family, and the habits and skills that would prepare my children for the real world. This included not only money but also the knowledge contained in all the books I've written, along with the skills I've learned as an investor and entrepreneur. Philanthropy is a key component in my family's legacy, too. I want you to think about what you want your legacy to represent and to share that with your family. As part of that process, interspersed throughout the chapters, you will find suggestions and tools to help you to either begin your estate planning or fine-tune it.

My mission is to help people build happy families who can grow in love together while learning how to tackle the challenges that life throws at us. I want to teach others how to become financially independent so that they're not dependent on others and can opt out of the system. But I also want people to embrace their soul purpose and live a life of abundance instead of constantly fighting the scarcity mindset.

People with financial intelligence can change the world for the better!

Welcome to *Happy Money, Happy Family, Happy Legacy.*

PART 1

FOUNDATIONS OF HAPPY MONEY

CHAPTER ONE

THE PHILOSOPHY OF MONEY

If we command our wealth, we will be rich and free.
If our wealth commands us, we are poor indeed.
−Richard Burke

It was yet another week of not getting paid. I was standing in the empty parking lot on a Friday night, shivering in near-whiteout conditions thanks to yet another snowstorm making the roads impassible—meaning my restaurant would be doing zero business. I remember reaching into the bucket of calcium chloride with my gloveless hands and flinging it in frustration across the parking lot as I finished shoveling.

Friday night was when we made the big bucks, the night we relied on to cover our weekly expenses. Instead of a busy night, though, I was out in my parking lot all alone, wondering whether I was going to be able to cover the week's payroll.

These winters seem to be getting longer and longer. When will I make enough money to be happy? And is money ever going to make me happy? Is there an exit to this rat race that I'm running?

That's how it felt as owner of my Italian restaurant in New York. The restaurant was named Gino's Trattoria, after my grandfather. My family bought it back in 1994, and things went well for a while. The business did great! But things started to change in 2008, and the business began slumping. And as it slumped, so did I.

I had conditioned myself to tie my happiness to success: the amount of money that I was making and the things that I was buying. When business was great, I felt happier; I was in a better mood, and there was hope in the air. However, when business is great in the restaurant industry, it means you're working really hard, including on holidays and weekends.

When business wasn't great, I was grumpier and, to be honest, not too fun to be around. Things had gotten to the point where they were affecting my family life. How was I going to pay for six college tuitions, six weddings, cars, vacations, and—if my money lasted that long—retirement? Those were the things that I kept hearing—having a large family meant you needed a lot of money so that you could take care of them. That was my focus.

I've undergone an incredible journey in my relationship with money since that desperate, lonely time in the parking lot. Through investing with my business partner, Jake, and becoming financially free, I realized that money is just a *tool*. It's a means to an end. It's an inanimate object that's somehow capable of seizing our imagination and pulling so much emotion from us. Given that money plays so many roles—economic and emotional—before we go any further, we should take a moment and really consider what money is.

What Is Money?

Let's start by defining "money." Money is any object that's generally accepted as payment for goods, services, and repayment of debts in a given country or socio-economic context. The main functions of money are acting as a medium of exchange, a unit of account, a store of value, and, occasionally, a standard of deferred payment.

Now, can money bring you happiness? I think money can bring you a level of comfort, certainly, and when you spend it, you get a short-term dopamine hit that provides a nice jolt of energy, albeit brief.

However, I believe that *happiness* is derived from achieving autonomy—being able to have total control over your life and the decisions that you make. The more control you have, the better your quality of life.

Looking back on my restaurant days, I see now that I was unhappy for a few reasons. My father passed away in 2007; I had worked with him since I was eight years old. After his death, I began to question whether running the restaurant was his dream or my dream. But more importantly, I didn't have control over my time. I needed to be at the restaurant. I had to work on days when everyone else was having fun. I felt as if I had no future; I felt trapped. In essence, I didn't have autonomy over my decisions or my time.

When I became financially free, I no longer had to work at the restaurant to pay my monthly bills. I could choose to work with whomever, whenever, wherever, and for whatever reason I wanted. I remember thinking, "Once I become financially free, I'm gonna retire and sit on a beach and do nothing."

Boy, was I wrong about that one! My wife knew before I did that my retirement was going to be short-lived. I'd finally found my calling, investing in real estate and starting an educational company called Jake & Gino to teach people to invest in apartments. My joy came from helping others, becoming a life coach, and finding what my soul purpose was. Making more money is now just a byproduct of doing a great job.

Another activity that increased my happiness was donating to various charities. My family started working with the Franciscan Friars of the Renewal. They're a Catholic organization of brothers and priests who work with the poor. That's their mission. Every Thanksgiving, I would go down to their friary in Harlem and cook for their entire neighborhood.

Now, we were cooking turkeys for over 150 people, a costly endeavor. But that donation and that time spent in the community helping others has brought me so much joy and become something I have a true passion for doing.

I also created a company culture that employees wanted to be a part of. When I had the restaurant, I always felt like people were primarily working because they needed a paycheck. In the company that I have now, my employees show up for a better reason. They see the mission we're pursuing and the culture that we've created, and they want to create an impact in other people's lives. That's what's inspired me to create Jake & Gino and dedicate myself to the mission we've laid out. That mission is to create communities that empower people to be the best version of themselves. Our core values are **People First, Extreme Ownership, Make It Happen, Growth Mindset,** and **Unwavering Ethics.**

The final thing that I'll mention that's really increased my happiness is not stressing about paying basic bills, such as routine dental work. I remember a sad story from years ago when we didn't have a lot of money. My wife came to me one day and said, "Hey Gino, I need to get some work done on my teeth; it's going to cost a couple thousand dollars."

My reaction was, "Pfft, I'm not going to pay for that."

I'm so embarrassed to talk about it today. My wife desperately needed that dental work, and I couldn't come up with a couple thousand dollars to take care of her. But that's the beautiful thing about life and the journey that we're on. I'm not the same person that I was ten years ago; I'd be embarrassed to say that I was. Hopefully, ten years from now, I won't be the same person that I am today.

It's all about the growth. It's all about the awareness. It's all about the journey that we're on.

I came to realize that freedom and choice are so much more important than money. Money was just the result of my actions—the better I was in my work, the more money I made. But I also realized that I was not *chasing* money anymore. I had been chasing money at the restaurant because I had to pay the bills. I had to be there. Now, I'm chasing *opportunities*, and those opportunities turn into money.

Happy Money

Now that we've defined money, what is "happy money"? To me, happy money is money that enters or exits your life, brings a smile to your face, makes you feel joyful, is used to create an impact in other people's lives, and makes you feel grateful. Happy money attracts other happy money, and you feel empowered spending happy money.

There's an abundance mindset with happy money. It's money you don't worry about spending. *It's okay; I'm gonna make more money.* When I jump on a coaching call and help a Jake & Gino member, or I get an email from a member saying they've closed on a deal, or I help them save money in a deal, I'm energized, and I can feel that happy money flowing. Athletes call it being "in the zone." Entrepreneurs call it being "in the money" or "the value zone."

Money is just a byproduct of value creation—provide value to your customers, and you'll get paid. Provide more value to more customers, and you'll make more money.

Conversely, unhappy money is money that enters your life with negative energy, is spent unwillingly, and has scarcity attached to it. Even for people who say they have to save for a rainy day … why is it a *rainy* day? Why can't it be a sunny day at the beach? Are we being conditioned to save for a happy event or a catastrophe?

Even the way we teach our kids about saving is unhealthy. "Let me take the money you got as a birthday present, and I'll put it somewhere in a faraway place for you to one day maybe use." To a six-year-old, that just means you've taken away their money. What do you think happens when they become an adult and are told to save money? It's going to feel like a form of punishment.

Here's an example to illustrate unhappy money. If you despise going to work, but make the excuse that you *have* to, then the money you're earning is unhappy money. Remember me in the parking lot? That's how I was. If we continue to live in the world of unhappy money, what do you think will happen in our lives? We all have to get used to spending *and* saving money, so you might as well start figuring out how to create happy money.

What if we could look at this process in a different way? Wayne Dyer was famous for saying, "If you change the way you look at things, the way you look at things changes." That's exactly what I had to do when I thought about money. I had to challenge my internal biases and create a new appreciation for spending money.

We filter the world around us subconsciously in many different ways. But if we become aware of this filter, we can learn to challenge it. This will help us improve our relationship with money. The goal is to cut out mental limitations so we're free to explore, learn, and grow.

Changing Your Perception

I want to give you several examples of unhappy money in my life. By using Wayne's advice, I was able to change my perception and come to see them as happy money.

I dreaded paying certain bills around the house, such as a cleaning lady or a pool cleaner. I could choose *not* to pay for these services, but they did save me time and allowed me to focus on other activities that I enjoyed.

One thing we all need to pay for is electricity. Now, I own several properties, so these bills can add up. Plus, when you have a big home with six kids around all day because they homeschool, electricity bills can become pretty painful. One day, I was reading an article about Iraq and how they had rolling blackouts, and it reminded me of every time we had a big storm up in New York, and *we* lost power. What a pain! Food spoiling, being stuck at home in the dark, not being able to do anything …

At that moment, I realized a new appreciation for having electricity, and I decided to look at that expense as happy money. I changed the way I looked at it, and the electricity bill changed for me. I started to appreciate it more; in fact, I even started to feel thankful for it.

I started to do this with other expenses such as piano lessons, singing lessons, and the landscaper. I also realized that my enjoyment of these services began to grow, and an appreciation that I could afford them came about.

The word that I'm looking for here is *gratitude*. I wasn't thrilled that I had to part with my money, but I was grateful that I had a coach who could teach me how to sing opera and that someone showed up every week to cut my grass and make my house look great.

This is what money is about. Remember, it's a tool to be used for your enjoyment, not to be hoarded and worshipped. The irony is that those who save and scrimp all their lives for retirement are the ones who won't spend any of it or will feel tormented when they need to. That's the height of unhappy money and the height of the scarcity mindset.

To sum up, money is a tool—use the tool to help you buy experiences. Use the tool for happy money. Money is a result, and the better you get at something, the more the money will show up. Don't work for the money; work for opportunities and to create value, and money will show up for you.

The Game of Money

Money is a game, and it has rules. We're going to go over those rules in detail in a later chapter. For now, it's enough to understand that, like any other sport, it has rules, and you need to follow them. If you're playing football, you're not going to use a tennis racket; that would make you fail at the sport. So we'll learn what those rules of money are.

Now, let's move on to your next steps. The **first step** is for you to challenge your relationship with money. What are your beliefs about it? Have you hoarded your money and been afraid to enjoy it? Or have you been extremely happy with your money, but now the money is no longer there?

Take some time with this because it's important. Don't beat yourself up, but do be honest. This is a time to reflect. Sit with the emotions that will emerge and try to understand where they come from. The work is difficult, but I promise that *not* doing the work is even worse in the long run. As you do this exercise, you might feel regret, anger, frustration—that's all right. There's no judgment here. We all have our own biases.

My revelation came in 2008 when I picked up a book by T. Harv Eker called *Secrets of the Millionaire Mind*. I was so frustrated with my situation at the restaurant, but blamed everyone else, not me. Then, I got to one particular line in the book: "Your fruits are in your roots." It seems amazing that so few words could have such a profound, life-changing impact, but they did. Those words hit like lightning, illuminating a new path. I carried so many limiting beliefs, but my life changed when I decided to become responsible for everything in my life, including my thoughts. That's the lesson the book shared with me. It taught me to take ownership of my own mind.

Now, I was fortunate to go to life coaching school after that and become a certified life coach. That's when I really began to explore my limiting beliefs and ask myself those tough questions.

The **second step** in mastering your relationship with money is to start a conversation with your spouse and with your children so you can see what their views are. My wife, I like to joke, became financially free on August 30, 1998, the day we got married. After that, her thoughts—and therefore her worries—about money were simply non-existent. She stayed home, homeschooled the kids, and took care of the household. That was her focus. *My* focus and my thoughts, day and night, were about providing for the family and making money.

But these differences didn't pop into existence on the day of our marriage. Instead, we came into our relationship with vastly different thoughts about money. I was taught that money was to be saved, invested, and enjoyed. But money was rarely spoken of in her childhood household. Her mother was a very hard worker, but at the end of the week, it always seemed as if there was no money left over. That's the environment my wife grew up in. She didn't want the responsibility of thinking about money, and she didn't even know how to start talking about money. She had no frame of reference and only saw it as a bad thing.

When I told my wife that I wanted to become financially free, she didn't understand what that meant at first. When I started describing to her what financial freedom meant to me—"I can work whenever I want, wherever I want; I can fly your family down here to Florida for vacations, and we can pay for things and not have to struggle to cover something like braces"—I think a light bulb went off. She finally understood my side of the story.

If you're talking about money with your spouse or family and experiencing all the emotions and the energy it brings up, do your best to make yourself explicitly understood. Don't have any biases, and listen without any judgment to your spouse and your children. Make the discussion crystal clear—be honest and open, especially about your personal experiences and your upbringing.

Now, the **third step** is to start to look at things differently and begin to adopt that attitude of gratitude. *Thank you, God, for providing electricity. Thank you for having Amazon be able to print this book. Thank you for the people who helped me put this book together.* Gratitude can brighten your outlook, invigorate your mood, and help you feel more positive throughout the day to help you tackle challenges and shift your thoughts away from negative emotions.

The **last step** is to think about the concept of scarcity versus abundance in your life. Where does the scarcity mindset show up? In your family life? In your finances? Find where you notice it most and start challenging it because living a life with a mindset of abundance, not scarcity, is a surefire path to happiness.

CHAPTER TWO

THE PSYCHOLOGY OF MONEY AND HAPPINESS

Your input determines your outlook.
–Zig Ziglar

The year was 2008. My father had just passed away, and I was beginning to re-evaluate my life. Some would call it a mid-life crisis; I called it a crisis of values. I started to ask myself: Was owning a restaurant my dream or my father's dream? I had been working with him since I was eight years old, and I loved working with him. I admired the pride that he took in his job, his work ethic, the respect that he garnered in his position, and the excellence that he brought to being a chef. However, I felt as if I wasn't living up to his standards.

This is when I read T. Harv Eker's *Secrets of the Millionaire Mind*. As I read the book, I was angered by Eker at first. I think the word they use today is "triggered." Who did he think he was? Why was he calling me out and placing the blame on me for my shortcomings? He didn't know me or my personal situation.

After I calmed down, I took the time to reflect upon what Eker was really saying. Remember the line I mentioned in the last chapter, the one that stuck with me? It was "Your fruits are in your roots." What we see on the outside are the fruits, the achievements, the hard work, and the successes. But what creates good fruit? It's the roots, and mine were terrible and shallow. I didn't have the skills to be able to create the fruits that I wanted.

Moreover, I was blaming everyone else for the unhappy situation I found myself in. It was the president's fault, or it was the economy. It was the business, or it was my family. But once I realized that where I was in life at that particular moment was the result of all *my* actions up to that point in time, it dawned on me: I, and only I, was responsible for the outcomes in my life. From that day forward, I decided to take 100 percent responsibility for all my actions and to stop playing the victim card.

I joined a mentorship program in 2008 to learn to invest in real estate—specifically, multifamily real estate. A year before that, I couldn't have fathomed spending $25,000 on a program. Now, I saw that it was necessary to invest that money in myself in order to grow stronger roots. That's where my journey with happy money started. Instead of viewing the program as an expense, I viewed it as an investment toward my future.

I continued to dive into personal development and became very conscious of my inputs. I drove around in my car listening to Zig Ziglar, Tony Robbins, Jim Rohn, and Napoleon Hill, to name a few. I took to heart that my inputs determined my outlook, and I needed to fill my life with positive messages.

My situation didn't change overnight, of course. In fact, in 2008, I was driving my father's car to save on a car payment. When that car decided to die on me, it was on to my mom's hand-me-down. I went eight years without a car payment! All this time, my mindset was getting stronger. I was getting more accustomed to adversity, and my response was much different than it had been when I started my journey of self-education. I started to look for opportunities within a problem instead of just focusing on the problem itself.

Then, Jake showed up in my life in 2009. Was our connection the result of luck, or was it preparation? I'll let you decide. All I know is that if I hadn't had the knowledge of multifamily investing, aka strong roots, I wouldn't have been able to capitalize on Jake moving to Knoxville, Tennessee, in 2011. I wouldn't have been able to partner with him and provide value to him in our business endeavors.

My investment in myself didn't stop in 2008; that's when it *started*, and it only accelerated as the more I grew as an investor and entrepreneur, the more I realized how little I knew and how much more I needed to learn. Unfortunately, most of us feel as if some people are born with inherent talents that make them natural-born salespersons, leaders, or sports figures. That's the *furthest* thing from the truth. I wasn't born an entrepreneur, and neither was Jake—he was a pharmaceutical rep. Yet I went from owning one restaurant for over 20 years to, within five years of my investing journey, owning over 1,000 apartment units with Jake.

It comes down to one word: **mindset**!

In fact, the other book that changed the trajectory of my life is *Mindset*, written by Carol Dweck. In the book, she discusses the two mindsets: the fixed mindset and the growth mindset. In a fixed mindset, a person is static or "fixed." They feel the need to constantly prove themselves in all situations but are never at fault when things don't work out.

People with growth mindsets, on the other hand, believe that they can improve or change their traits over time. They see challenges as opportunities and are willing to make mistakes to learn.

A quick example of someone with a fixed mindset is the tennis star John McEnroe. He was an unbelievable talent who took to anger and blame when things didn't go his way. It was never *his* fault.

It was either the sawdust, the wind, the crowd noise, or his racket. That's what the fixed mindset does: it looks for excuses.

To contrast that, I would use Michael Jordan as someone with a growth mindset. Anyone who follows basketball knows that Michael Jordan was cut from his high school basketball team his sophomore year, but did he quit? No—he continued to practice and get better, and he ultimately ended up winning six NBA championships.

One important aspect of fixed and growth mindsets is that you can have a fixed mindset in one area of your life and a growth mindset in another area. An area of my life at the time where I was experiencing a growth mindset was in raising my family. We were bucking conventional wisdom by homeschooling, and it was working extremely well for us. Our children were thriving at home, I was able to spend more time with them, and in turn, they were able to spend more time among themselves. If my fixed mindset had reared its ugly head, I would have probably felt the pressure to send them to school. Looking back, I have to give my wife most of the credit. Her conviction and passion convinced me to trust her.

But at the time I picked up T. Harv Eker's book, I was severely entrenched in the fixed mindset when it came to business and personal development. I fit all the fixed characteristics: unwilling to grow, sensitive to criticism, and blaming others.

Now, I want to ask you: where are you exhibiting a fixed mindset? Is it about money, relationships, or your job? It's never too late to begin to adopt a growth mindset. The first step is awareness, which is what you're working on right now. The next step is the willingness to humble yourself and admit that there's so much in life to learn. What helped me was changing my perspective so that I saw life as a beautiful journey and not so much as a destination to shoot for. I was on my own path of growth, and I tried to stop comparing my journey to others.

The Three Money Mindsets

Let's move on to the mindsets of money. The three mindsets are

1. Poor
2. Middle Class
3. Wealthy

Keep in mind that mindset has nothing to do with the amount of money you earn per year. I know plenty of people with a poor mindset who are earning high-six-figure incomes and yet living paycheck to paycheck. Instead, look at these mindsets as a set of characteristics or habits.

Additionally, I'm not judging any one mindset to be better than another right now. I'm only trying to point out the differences so that you can become aware of them and choose which one you ultimately want to adopt.

People with a **poor mindset** have no regard for the future and spend money as quickly as they make it, exhibiting a fixed mindset around money. They think that the solution to their money problems is to make more money. Their language around money is also fixed, saying things such as "I can't afford it," or "Do you think money grows on trees?" They're stuck in the scarcity mindset, aka unhappy money.

The **middle-class mindset** has been conditioned to save for events, such as college tuition for their kids, 401(k)s and retirement. They have been trained by society to keep up with the Joneses and often carry significant personal debt to portray the illusion of wealth and success. I was trapped in the middle-class mindset before I began investing with Jake, with the exception of high personal debt, which I had very little of. When I reflect back, I find it interesting to see how I was a mixture of the poor mindset, with scarcity in my life, and the middle-class mindset, with having to save for so many different events.

Then there's the **wealthy mindset**. One of the most important characteristics of the wealthy mindset is that these people are
responsible for their lives. They have a concrete, solid plan, and they
focus on what they want in their lives versus what they don't want.
When I was at the restaurant, I was asked, "Well, what do you want
to do?" I was quick to say that I didn't want to be at the restaurant,
but that wasn't the question. The question was, "What do you *want?*"
but I didn't really have a clue.

The wealthy mindset focuses on solutions. They have a healthy
relationship with money and understand how to attract happy money into their lives. They value relationships over money. They are
charitable with their happy money. Ultimately, their goal is to provide value and chase opportunities, and those opportunities end up
attracting happy money. Wealthy people are producers, and from
their production, they spend and invest their money. Contrast this
with the poor mindset, who is a consumer only and has no thoughts
on producing anything.

Money Personas

Now that we have an understanding of the money mindsets, let's explore your **money persona**. What is a money persona? It's a personality or trait that drives your financial and monetary decisions.
There are five main money personas, each with different beliefs, actions, and relationships with money. Let's take a look at each one:

1. **Steve the Saver:** He's focused on saving, and money is al-
    ways scarce. He uses phrases like, "It's not the right time"
    or "It's just not in the budget." Steve doesn't like to spend
    money on himself and has very little happy money. Huh! He
    sounds a bit like how I used to be.
2. **Sara the Spender:** Her happiness and self-worth are tied
    to portraying a lavish lifestyle. Her happy money comes from

spending it all, but then she's left with the fear of where more money will come from.

3. **Amy the Avoider:** Money is a foreign language to Amy, and she avoids talking about it at all costs. She doesn't look at her bank or credit card statements, and she possesses a scarcity mindset with money. It's difficult to attract happy money when you're trying to avoid it altogether.

4. **George the Gambler:** George is always moving from one venture to the next with the promise of hitting it big. Jake and I call this "shiny object syndrome," where George starts out investing in real estate, sees very little progress, and jumps onto crypto, where he's sure to hit it big. Once crypto fails, he's off to the next thing that's caught his attention.

5. **Ivan the Investor:** Ivan's sole focus is to earn money and to continue to grow his empire. It may appear that Ivan is living in the land of happy money, but he *can't enjoy* his money because his sole focus is to make more of it.

In reality, most of us have a dominant money persona, but we also have pieces of all five personas. Early on, I was Steve the Saver with a bit of Amy when the restaurant business was slow. I embraced Ivan right after reading T. Harv Eker's book and have slowly adopted Sara's habit of spending money to enjoy it, even on myself.

The key to changing your relationship with money is to identify which money type you are now, what persona you would like to align with more, and begin to look at money through the lens of happy versus unhappy. I thought the Ivan money persona would bring me happy money, but I realized that I wasn't enjoying my money. What's the purpose of strengthening your roots if you can't enjoy the fruit?

One vital way to understand your relationship to money and your money persona is to go back to your childhood and reflect upon what you heard, what you experienced, and what you were taught about money.

I vividly remember one day going food shopping with my Grandma Anna. When we got to the grocery store, I saw a bag of toy soldiers, and all of a sudden, I *needed* to buy them right then and there. Grandma told me that she only had enough money to buy the groceries—back then, there were no credit cards—but she assured me that as soon as we got home and my mom came to pick me up, she and I would go back and buy them. I knew we wouldn't, though.

I still remember the sadness in my grandmother's face when she couldn't buy those soldiers for me and the despair that I felt. What I learned that day was that I needed to save money, that it was terrible not to be able to afford something, and that money was scarce. I also learned to equate accomplishing something with doing it immediately, or else the opportunity would be lost forever.

Another example of acquiring behavior from family and friends is when I got married. Instead of buying a nice, affordable starter home and investing the rest of my money, I decided to build a 3,500-square-foot home. Two years later, I sold that home to build another home right next to my restaurant. This home was 4,500 square feet!

Looking back, it would have made so much more financial sense to sell the first home and buy the second home as a fixer-upper. I would have saved a lot of money by not building another brand-new home, and I wouldn't have felt the pressure to upkeep the new home so much.

Huh, where did that thinking about needing to build big new homes come from? It took a while for me to unpack it, but eventually, I did. When I went back to Italy to visit family, it was clear that their home was their castle; they viewed their wealth in terms of their house and their land. I had adopted these beliefs from my mom, along with the pressure to keep up appearances. Their view on money was that you were investing in an asset, and your home was your future.

No wonder I went big. If I had been aware of these biases and the hold that my past had on me, I would have made a different decision and bought the fixer-upper.

The Four Happy Hormones

Before we continue, let's dive into some neuroscience and explore how the brain affects our ability to save and spend money. After all, if we're trying to change our thoughts and mindsets, we should understand how that process works in our brains. Here are the **four happy hormones** and why they're so important for creating happy money.

1. First up is **dopamine**. It's called a feel-good hormone or the rewarding hormone, and when released, it can improve your mood and make you feel good. Now, if you have a spender persona, you derive pleasure from going out and spending. Even the *thought* of spending releases dopamine. That quick rush makes you feel great, but soon after, the feeling is gone. You're left with a purchase that made you feel good for a short period of time, but now you're beating yourself up for wasting money.

Many of our decisions or habits are the result of wanting that dopamine hit. If you're stressed, you may reach for the fridge, grab a cigarette, buy some lotto tickets, or go work out. The habits that you create will decide whether you are creating happy or unhappy money. When I was stressed, looking at my bank account would alleviate the stress, so I was subconsciously telling myself not to spend money and to continue to save.

2. The second happy hormone is **endorphins**. These are created when we need to respond to pain or stress. They are

often called pain killers. They help you overcome stress or discomfort and are produced during pleasurable activities.

3. The third happy hormone is **serotonin**. It's called the mood stabilizer, and it's linked to pride, confidence, and respect. It works by regulating mood levels and happiness.

4. The final happy hormone is **oxytocin**. This is commonly referred to as the love hormone, and it's vital for strong parent-child bonding.

You may be saying to yourself, "Why do I need to understand these hormones, and how will this help me create happy money?" These hormones regulate your mood, and if you are under constant stress, live in scarcity, and have constant negative thoughts, it will be extremely difficult to see or attract happy money.

There is good news, though. You can produce more of these happy hormones right now. How can you do it?

1. Firstly, get outside. Take a lovely walk in nature and expose yourself to the sun. A nice 15-minute walk on the beach shifts my mood completely.

2. Exercise, whatever kind you like. You can even consider working out with friends. I love playing tennis with my kids. Whatever exercise you can be committed to, do it.

3. Spend time within a community of people. It's amazing to see the community at Jake & Gino when we get together at onsite events—talk about happy hormones!

4. Laughter or even a smile. Try it as you're reading this—it's amazing how a change in your physiology can change your psychology.

5. Music. Ever since I began singing opera, I have seen the effect Franco Corelli has had on my mood throughout the day. Just listening to music is incredibly uplifting to me.

6. Meditate/pray. This is an incredible way to slow down the day and practice gratitude.
7. Breathe. Just focus on your breathing for a while—you might try something like the Wim Hof method. Simply being conscious of your breathing can be a great way to slow down and relax.
8. Sleep. There have been so many studies on how the lack of sleep can be incredibly detrimental to your overall health— shoot for seven to eight hours a night.
9. Diet/supplementation. Remember how your input determines your outlook? It's so important to take care of your diet in order to help you regulate your happy hormones.

Ultimately, you're trying to limit the amount of stress you're under and learn how to deal with that stress more effectively. Chronic stress often leads to inflammation, which, if not dealt with, will lead to a much lower quality of life, sickness, and eventually death.

When we're young, we can get away with some bad habits like overeating, drinking a bit too much, and not sleeping enough. But I can tell you, if you want to continue to attract happy money, you need to focus on your health and well-being.

If you are constantly visiting doctors or worried about your health, your preoccupied mind won't be able to focus on much else effectively. Please don't make excuses that you don't have the time to exercise or eat properly. I had a health scare back in 2017, and the fear, worry, and anxiety from it consumed me for a time.

In one way, that scare was a good thing. I stopped taking things for granted, and I started appreciating life and my family a lot more. On the other hand, the time spent away from home and the uncertainty I was facing were very challenging.

Now, my stress never goes away completely—I have six kids, businesses, and so many other obligations—but I will tell you that I felt much more stressed years ago when I had a fraction of the responsibilities. I've become aware of my stress and adopted the habits that I listed above to help me manage that stress.

iPEC and Energy Blocks

One of the most profound experiences for my personal development journey, if not *the* most profound, was becoming a Certified Life Coach in 2014. I attended the Institute for Professional Excellence in Coaching (iPEC) not for the degree but to learn the skills of a life coach and to use them for myself. Not only has it transformed *my* life, but my wife saw my transformation and decided to get certified as well. Next in line were my two oldest children, and I'm so proud of them all.

When I decided to attend iPEC, I was in the midst of working at the restaurant, plus expanding it to include a winery in the next town, in the process of purchasing our third multifamily deal, and had a pregnant wife with child number six on the way. Drinking out of a fire hose was the understatement of the year, but my growth mindset found a way to tackle all of these obligations.

The reason I share this with you is that I learned about mindset, and specifically something called an "energy block," at iPEC. Little did I know that back in 2008, but my life was filled with energy blocks.

What is an energy block? It's something that holds you back, whether internal (your thoughts and beliefs) or external (the economy). I bet you wouldn't believe me if I told you that the vast majority of your energy blocks are internal. That's what I want to focus on right now. Getting over these blocks is the key to attracting and living a life with happy money.

Jim Kwik, the author of *Limitless*, is famous for saying that your behaviors are belief-driven. If you think you can, then you can. Your brain is there to prove you right.

The first energy block that I want to share is what is referred to as a "limiting belief." A limiting belief is something that you accept about your life or yourself that limits you in some capacity. In the context of money, I was loaded with limiting beliefs. "It takes money to make money," "Real estate is risky," "I can't afford it," "I'm too late to the game," "I'm too young or old," and on and on. If you believe your limiting beliefs, you are unlikely to take action to conquer them. I needed to actually look around and see others who were successful (who weren't trust fund babies) and were succeeding in real estate.

If you take the time to look up the men and women who started some of the largest businesses in the world, most started out with little to no money. What they had was a solution to a problem in the marketplace and value they could provide to their investors. Take your pick of amazing entrepreneurs: Steve Jobs of Apple, Michael Dell of Dell Computers, Howard Schultz of Starbucks, Sarah Blakely of Spanx, and Oprah Winfrey. They all came onto the scene with little backing but a lot of belief, and they turned the business world on its head with their successes.

I wasn't convinced until my limiting belief was shattered on the first deal I did with Jake when we bought a 25-unit complex with seller financing. Seller financing is a creative financing technique in real estate where the seller provides either the entire down payment in the form of a "seller-financed note" or a partial down payment. The note is treated as a mortgage, and the buyer typically makes monthly payments to the seller. The sellers utilize seller financing when it is difficult to finance a property with traditional lending or when the property is in distress, and the seller is motivated to sell.

In our situation, we purchased the property for $600,000. The bank provided us with 80 percent of the down payment ($480,000), the seller held a note for $60,000, and we had to provide a total of $83,000, which included closing costs. Let's put this into the perspective of my mind's limiting belief. We had control of a $600,000 asset for only $83,000 out of our pocket, yet we still controlled 100 percent of the benefits: the cash flow, the appreciation, and the tax benefits. From that point on, I shattered the limiting belief of needing to have money to make money.

In fact, two years later, we closed on an $11 million property with seller financing. The seller provided the entire 20 percent down payment, and the bank provided the remaining 80 percent. You might be saying this is too good to be true, and I would have agreed with you back in 2011. But not anymore!

The good news with limiting beliefs is that once you can prove to yourself that they're false, they can be easily surmounted. If you'd like to learn more about creative financing, check out our book *Creative Cash*, which dives into buying real estate using creative financing techniques. You can find the book here: *Creative Cash*.

What limiting beliefs are showing up in your life? What ones are you holding on to? Now ask yourself, "How true is that belief? What evidence do I have to support that belief? How has that belief affected me, and how can I let it go?"

The next energy block that I want to focus on has a huge hold on many of us. With a limiting belief, it's just a belief. But with this block, you've actually experienced it—it's a part of your DNA. At iPEC, it is called an "Assumption." Essentially, it is an expectation that because something has happened in the past, it will reoccur in the future.

When I learned about Assumptions, I literally began to cry. It brought me back to my first partnership in real estate, and how it ended in disaster, with me losing my entire investment. It took years for the wound to heal. Fortunately for me, by the time I partnered with Jake, I had done enough work on my assumptions that I refused to let this one hold me back.

I see people hesitating to invest in real estate, start a business, or even go out on a date because their previous attempts ended in failure, leaving them convinced that the next attempt will yield the same result. How do we overcome Assumptions? Ask this question: "Just because it happened in the past, why *must* it happen again?" I asked myself that question when I decided to partner with Jake, and it was one of the best things I've ever done for myself.

I've begun to live by the quote, "Your external appearances are a manifestation of what's going on inside." Simply put, your thoughts create your results.

As we wrap up this discussion on personal development and happiness, I'd be remiss if I didn't bring the emotion of anger into the conversation. Anger is a powerful emotion that can overtake our lives, and yet most of us tell ourselves that we're not angry. Wikipedia has a great definition of anger:

> *"An intense emotional state involving a strong uncomfortable an non-cooperative response to a perceived provocation, hurt, or threat."*

It took me years to fully understand the destructive nature of anger and the impact it could have on my life if I didn't begin to confront it.

I attended a personal development event called Brave Soul, hosted by Philip McKernan, and one of the questions he asked was, "On a scale of 1–10, how angry are you?" When I was first asked the question, my response was a 2. Actually, almost everyone in the room had the same response.

I'm not an angry person. Sure, sometimes I lose my cool, but I'm a happy guy who has everything under control. I kept telling myself that story until Philip made me confront the source of my anger. I admit, at the time, I was also under the impression that anger could be a *good* thing. It motivated me to get things done. It made me productive … but at what cost? I became very good over the years at suppressing my anger, or as some might say, managing my anger. What I came to realize is that when I was in a state of anger, I was also in a state of scarcity.

At Philip's event, we started off by looking into our childhood. It had been a while since I reminisced about my youth. At first, I thought my childhood was great. I was happy; my mom and dad were great. Everything was great. Then, the wheels started falling off the bus when I dug deeper. Although many parts of my childhood were, in fact, terrific, I'd also experienced quite a bit of trauma.

Of course, when I first heard Philip use the word trauma, I was steadfast and argued to myself that I was trauma-free. But truthfully, I *did* experience trauma in certain ways. First off, I was a chubby kid, and my size between 9 and 13 years old was "husky." I'm not kidding; they had a size called "husky" for kids that were overweight. I was often teased for my chubbiness, for lack of a better word. I *did* end up losing weight in high school, but the teasing, the shame, the criticizing, and the bullying stayed with me and sometimes still affects me to this day.

At home, my mother was very controlling and often became frustrated with us, which frequently resulted in the dreaded wooden spoon coming out or, even worse, a shoe flying across the room. What made it worse for me later on in life was that I felt guilty for being mad at my mother for spanking me. She was doing the best that she knew how, even though it wasn't the best for me.

I would also get blamed for occurrences in the home, even if I *wasn't* at fault. Now, to be fair, I wasn't an angel, but I often felt as if my mother didn't even listen to me. I remember one time in Italy, on a family vacation, when my cousin had my Walkman. Yes, I know, I'm dating myself. We got into an argument, and I wanted it back. My mother heard us arguing, and she came in swinging like a UFC fighter. Once she realized that it was mine, I could see the shame on her face. That was the last time she even spanked me.

I will be eternally grateful to Philip for what he calls "helping me do the work." As a life coach, I was trained to briefly look at your past, acknowledge where you are in the present, and create a plan for your future. You're always looking forward, but what Philip taught me is that you carry scars and trauma from your childhood, and if you don't confront them, they'll continue to control your actions. In my case, the emotion of anger kept popping up without me knowing why.

I would highly recommend reading Philip's book, *One Last Talk*, and if you're struggling with anger or want someone to talk to about your past, consider hiring a therapist. I found it life-changing when I was able to talk to someone about my past and work on my issues of anger. However, although therapy can be transformative, I've seen many people in therapy for years, stuck with the same problems and constantly dwelling on the past, not trying to work toward a solution. Many therapists focus on making sense of the past in the present, but they don't help you look forward to the future. Similarly, a life coach might be amazing at helping you visualize a fantastic future, but many aren't trained to help you revisit your past to see how the events of your childhood might affect your outlook—and your anger—today.

I knew that I didn't want to get stuck in the past, and Philip provided the perfect balance I was looking for. Once we relived the memories of our past, Philip took us on a beautiful journey of our present and then made us visualize and state what our future could look like.

Anger puts a person into a catabolic state, a draining, resisting type of energy that breaks things down rather than build new things. When we exhibit this catabolic energy, it puts us into a state of fight or flight. Some people use the word "triggered" when they become angry. They have an argument with someone, they get triggered, and the emotion of anger bubbles to the surface. Sometimes, it may be beneficial to "get angry" to motivate yourself. But it can be much too easy to stay in this state for too long.

I've experienced this many times, and one thing is certain: when I'm in this state, the scarcity mindset kicks in, and solutions fly out the window. You don't believe me? Think back to the last time this happened to you. Someone challenged your beliefs, and you got angry and tried to think of a response, but you drew a blank. You couldn't come up with any answers. You walked away, and ten minutes later, the answer popped into your head!

I had the privilege of interviewing a gentleman named Dr. Mort Orman, who wrote *Dr. Orman's Life Changing Anger Cure*. Now, I don't believe that you can eliminate your anger, as Dr. Mort does, but if you can begin to understand the root of your anger, you can then change your response to your anger.

I've shared several stories with you about my anger, and after speaking with Dr. Mort, it became clear that I was looking at these situations through my filters. I had a sort of built-in bias, and I was unable or unwilling to see the other side of the story. My hope is that when anger starts to build up inside of you, you can take a moment to think about the story you're telling yourself and challenge the story.

Steven Covey, author of *The 7 Habits of Highly Effective People*, discusses the stimulus-response theory, which states that we are conditioned to respond in a certain way to a certain stimulus. He states that in between our stimulus and response lies our greatest power: our ability to choose how to respond. An example of a stimulus response is touching a hot stove and then quickly removing your hand from the heat. In that case, the response is immediate and unconscious, meaning we do it without thought. But while our response to heat is automatic because it's a reflex to protect ourselves, other types of responses can become so ingrained that they feel like reflexes, too, and occur without thought.

When I am filled with anger, or I am looking at a situation through my filters, and then I'm stimulated, guess what happens? That space between stimulus and response is practically nonexistent, and my response isn't well thought out. I believe that one of the keys to making empowering decisions is to become aware of this space and to look at the situation through a broad lens. Give yourself the time to collect your thoughts—don't shoot back a quick text—and sit with the idea that you may be wrong in how you're assessing the situation.

You need to become aware of your internal filters, which are essentially lenses that color how you see and interpret things that happen. Dr. Mort states that there are three internal filters for generating your anger. I love the simplicity with which Dr. Mort tackles anger, and I feel compelled to share his three primary filters:

1. Someone or something did something "bad" or "wrong" they shouldn't have done.
2. Someone or something suffered harm, humiliation, embarrassment, offense, disappointment, inconvenience, or other negative consequences due to the actions taken.
3. The entity responsible for the "bad" or "wrong" action, which caused harm or negative consequences, bears 100 percent of the blame (unilateral blame) for both #1 and #2 above.

Dr. Mort's contention is that anger is caused by viewing your life's events through these internal filters.

Next, I would challenge you to walk through one of your latest anger episodes. I was recently flying back from one of our Jake & Gino events, and our flight got canceled. I was sitting in the airport at 11 p.m. on a Sunday night, waiting to fly home. Instead, I had to get a hotel room for the evening and be back at the airport in the morning.

If I apply Dr. Mort's framework, I can understand what caused my anger at the situation, along with how to respond to the anger. I was being hugely inconvenienced, along with thousands of other passengers. I was still pissed off, but when I reverted to his framework, I could see that the airline was not 100 percent responsible. The weather was wreaking havoc, and there were countless flights canceled. I was able to adjust my stimulus response accordingly, create a plan to get a ticket for the next day, and allow the anger to subside. I still got angry, but I was able to view it through a wider lens and create a solution, and more importantly, I wasn't stewing in that emotion for very long.

I think the key to being able to deal with your anger is to acknowledge or admit to yourself that you carry anger. For you to work on a problem, you need to be able to admit to yourself that the problem exists in the first place. I would follow up that realization by trying to identify what triggers you or where the anger originates. I've found that most of us love to beat ourselves up. *There I go again. I can't believe I just yelled at my spouse.* Please don't criticize yourself. You aren't the only one who wrestles with this emotion.

Start to become aware of the stimulus, the response, and the space in between. As you become more aware of the triggers and you use Dr. Mort's framework, you will be able to work through the emotion and create positive outcomes. To me, the key isn't to stop getting angry. It's to find out *why* I'm getting angry, how I can deal *effectively* with the emotion, and what I can do to create more empowering responses.

It's pretty hard to create happy money or a happy family if we're constantly battling the emotion of anger and lack a way to deal with it effectively. I don't want my legacy to be one of a grumpy or angry father.

There were times when I would come home feeling defeated from working at the restaurant. I would often get angry when there was a snowstorm or we lost power. It meant that I was working for free that week. Times like that infuriated me. One night, I remember driving home during a blizzard. I had been stuck at the restaurant alone on a Saturday night, and I had to drive home in over 18 inches of snow.

When I got home, my children were all so happy about the snow because it meant that the sleds were coming out in the morning. That night, I realized that I had no control over the weather, only how I reacted to it. I wasn't the only one affected by the weather either. Every other business owner in town faced the same fate. I decided to join the kids in fun that night, with hot chocolate by the fire and playing games together. The next day was followed by some of the best sleigh rides ever!

We all have the ability to choose how we act and how we want to be remembered. I choose to be a father who embraces responsibility and always tries to look for opportunities when problems arise. What do you want *your* legacy to be? Maybe now is the time to sit with it and decide how you want to be remembered.

Here are your next steps before moving on:

1. Identify areas in your life where you are exhibiting either a fixed or growth mindset. Don't judge yourself too harshly; just know that you have the choice to change. Where in your life do you want to pivot to a growth mindset?
2. What are your money mindset and money persona? The keys to change are to know where you currently are and to be aware and honest with yourself.
3. Start to become aware of your daily habits and whether or not they lead to the production of happy hormones. What could you change right now that would help you create more of these hormones?
4. Look at your belief system. As I mentioned earlier, your behaviors are belief-driven. If you think you can, you can. Your brain is there to prove you right. Look into life coaching and learn the benefits of either hiring a coach or becoming one to help drive this point home. And remember, if you need more help, you can contact me here: Gino Barbaro.

CHAPTER 3

PRACTICAL MONEY MANAGEMENT FOR THE FAMILY

If you can't measure it, you can't manage it.
–Peter Drucker

"Hey Dad, we just went over budget on the grocery bill this month," Michael said with excitement and surprise.

"What do you mean?" said his mom, Julia. "How do you even know that, and how much have we spent?!"

That was our introduction to family budgeting! We had just moved to Florida and were now living right across the street from a Publix. I kept seeing charges from Publix racking up, and I felt as if we were overspending. When you have a gut feeling or your intuition is telling you something, listen. So, I decided to start tracking our expenses.

When I was in the restaurant business, I rarely used credit cards. I even filled up my car at the gas station with cash, so I had a firm grip on my income and expenses. I was the last remnant of a generation that did not grow up with the internet, and I was unaccustomed to having recurring charges on my credit card. I knew what I spent.

When people want to lecture you about how difficult it is for the younger generation to save and to get ahead in this economy, there *is* merit to that argument, but I may have a differing opinion as to why. When I was growing up, we didn't have cell phone bills, a WiFi bill, Amazon, Spotify, Hulu, Ring, Disney, Netflix, and the countless other conveniences that are available today. Now, there are so many different places to spend money, and the ease with which you can get caught up in this spending frenzy can become dangerous to your financial well-being.

Jake likes to call it the S.A.T. (not the Scholastic Aptitude Test): Starbucks, Amazon, and Target. It's the joke in his household when he's looking at his credit card statement. This is the reality we live in.

When I was growing up, I had to wait an entire week to watch my favorite TV shows. Now, you can watch a whole season in a day. I had to suffer through commercials to listen to the music on the radio. Not anymore. Back then, we had to drive to the mall to buy clothes and books. Today, you can get almost anything shipped to your doorstep within 48 hours.

In a later chapter, we'll be discussing habits we can teach our kids to take control of reckless spending. It's not all about cutting things out; after all, some of these conveniences add tremendous value to our lives and can make us more efficient. For now, let's focus on how to teach our kids to create happy money habits so that they can decide where and how much money they want to spend on these luxuries.

So, where do we start with teaching our kids about money? Let me start with one of my biggest mistakes. Early on, I was extremely strict about teaching my kids about money, and it ended up being a

chore for them. Kids, as well as adults, learn best when they're playing games and being entertained, and it has to be age-appropriate.
Not all kids are created equal, and some will gravitate toward learning sooner than others.

Another piece of advice that I would give is to be consistent
with your actions and your advice to your kids. If you're telling
them the dangers of credit cards, yet you're routinely late with
your bill and spend money like a drunken sailor, your children will
smell the hypocrisy. It's taken me a while to be transparent with my
kids, but now I'll share the mistakes I made with them. I've even
learned how to say sorry to my kids. That was a tough one! More
on that in a later chapter.

When my kids were young, around the age of five, I started them
on the bucket system. I got empty plastic spice containers and placed
labels on them: Spending, Saving, Investing, and Charity. Why containers instead of the bank? I believe that kids need to see their money, have a say in how they use their money, and learn how to take
ownership of their money. I *did* open up bank accounts for each of
them to use when they received larger sums of money and when I
decided to save some money for them.

The savings account was also important because it was a way
to teach them about earning interest and the cost of money. They
were earning a return on their money while it was an expense to the
bank. What an amazing lesson to teach a child—that interest is the
cost of using money, but it can also become a way to generate happy
money for yourself.

Kids at this age need to see money as something tangible and
start learning what to do with it. The spending bucket was *their* money to enjoy. The saving bucket was a reserve fund. The investing
bucket was for opportunities, and the charity bucket was for them to
be able to donate to whatever cause they wanted to.

I'm less concerned with the percentages you decide to allocate
to each bucket and more concerned that you begin. Even at this

young age, it's appropriate to discuss bills and why Mom and Dad go to work.

As the kids get older, start playing games such as Life and Monopoly with them. My children accuse me of being competitive, but I disagree. I just don't like to lose! I started playing Monopoly with the kids when they were around seven years old. It's a great way for them to learn math and an easy introduction to the world of investing in real estate. Please buy the game with the money, not the version with credit cards. The game introduces concepts such as negotiation, mortgaging properties, collecting rent, and paying taxes. The key is to make it fun and to explain to them as you go along.

The only thing I don't like about Monopoly is the fact that the only way to win is to bankrupt the other players. I like the accumulation aspect, the investing in properties, but business and life aren't always a zero-sum game. One person doesn't always have to lose in a business transaction. The vast majority of my real estate purchases were beneficial to me, but the sellers ended up making money as well.

Once we played Monopoly for a few years, it was time to graduate to Robert Kiyosaki's Rich Dad CASHFLOW board game. For me, it was love at first play. It's a blend of teaching high-level concepts, along with incorporating real-life examples and having players battle to see who creates enough passive income from their investments to become financially free. As you sit with your child filling out a balance sheet, income statement, and statement of expenses, ask yourself: how many adults do you know who understand these financial statements? Your language becomes your experience, and the more comfortable your kids become with the language of personal finance, the less they'll have to fear as they get older.

Be patient with your kids when playing. Robert Kiyosaki has done a masterful job incorporating the world of finance into a board game. It's amazing to see kids adopt new habits when they start playing the game, such as not spending their money on luxuries (Rich

Dad calls them "doodads") and saving their money to buy assets that produce income. The goal is to teach kids these empowering habits while having fun as a family!

As you begin to build the foundation of happy money through playing games, I suggest also starting to introduce new vocabulary to them. If you've been playing the games, your kids will have heard the words personal financial statement, net worth, mortgage, and credit cards. When they hit their teenage years, start involving them in the day-to-day activities of maintaining your home. We decided to hire the kids to clean the home weekly. They learned so many great lessons like the importance of hard work, how it benefited them to not make as much of a mess during the week—and the fun of getting paid to do a job!

Another fun activity that I partake in is bringing the kids to the grocery store with only cash in my pockets. That's the only money we're allowed to use—no credit cards. The looks on their faces as we walk through the grocery store, calculating the cost of each item to make certain not to go over budget, makes me so proud.

This exercise achieves a few objectives. The first is that it's a great way to show your kids that you actually use math in every-day life. Try convincing a young teenager that they're going to use algebra as they get older. Good luck! But using math with money? Winner winner!

The second objective is that they see the actual cost of each item and can decide whether to purchase the more expensive organic crackers or the less expensive cookies. And, of course, they see that physical money is being used to buy food, not some plastic card, which really brings the lesson home that money is finite. It's a great way for them to begin to make decisions based on the resources they have at their disposal.

One area where I failed miserably when the kids were young was forcing them to read books on money and finance, even though the books were supposedly written for kids. Most *adults* find these books painfully boring and confusing. What was I thinking? I was just blessed to have an amazing wife who told me more than once that the kids hated it and that I should give up and wait until they got older.

One book I did have success with when they hit their teenage years was *The Richest Man in Babylon* by George S. Clason, a parable about a man who creates rules to become wealthy. My children also enjoyed the book Jake and I wrote called *The Honey Bee*, another parable about a man who discovers a mentor who teaches him how to create wealth. My wife has also authored three kids' books about money, relationships, and personal development. I'll be discussing our books in the chapter on legacy.

These books all have a few very important traits in common: they're written as stories, they're enjoyable to read, and they hold the reader's attention while delivering important messages about money and business. The worst thing that you can do is force your child to read something they don't like. You're closing the door on future conversations if you persist—or, at the very least, the door will be much harder to open once they come of age to need to put that knowledge into practice.

The key is to let the kids go at their own pace, not force them. Jake and I have just written a book called *Baby Money Soldiers*, which I'll go into in the next chapter. I have yet to share it with my younger children, but my 18-year-old just finished it. She enjoyed the book and found it to be entertaining and easy to understand. I was pleasantly surprised when my daughter told me she'd read it. Let me tell you, if there's hope for me when it comes to getting through to my kids, then there's hope for anyone!

Let's get back to Michael in the kitchen and his mother screaming that we went over budget—it was one of my proudest teachable moments. What made me so happy? I wasn't trying to punish my wife for overspending. I was trying to teach my children about the inflow and outflows of money in the family budget and how we could control those flows. We are responsible for what we want to spend and what we want to spend our money on.

The tool that I used to help our family track our money is called EveryDollar, a program created by Dave Ramsey. This one has worked well for us, but there are a lot of options out there. I recommend using any tool that you find easy and intuitive as long as you can stick with it.

Soon after the kitchen encounter, I decided to apply for a Costco membership. I also started shopping at Walmart for groceries and other household items. We've actually ended up saving tens of thousands of dollars a year. That may seem like an exaggeration, but I *do* have six children who love to eat!

I think a budget is a crucial element when it comes to creating happy money and teaching children about money, although I prefer to call it a spending plan rather than a "budget," which sounds restrictive and limiting. My view is that your home should be run similarly to a business. What business do you know that's truly successful that doesn't have a solid grasp on their finances, their profit and loss statements, their statement of cash flows, and their income statement?

Once again, be mindful of the child's age when you introduce a spending plan. My son Michael was 15 years old when I had him inputting numbers into ours. He already had a solid foundation and understood income and expenses. Involving him empowered him, and I was helping him form the habit so that when he became an adult, he'd be able to create his own spending plan.

Fast forward seven years, and he's graduating college, has invested in six of my multifamily deals, started his own LLC and business, and works monthly with our bookkeeper to maintain his records. Without his strong foundation, he never would've had the confidence to invest his own money and start a business.

I've been there every step of the way, guiding him through his investments and showing him how to fill out his Personal Financial Statement (PFS). However, when he asked me about a business license or a sales tax certificate, I told him I had never gotten them by myself. I had always used my accountant. To my amazement, he applied for and received them on his own.

I decided not to help him because I wanted him to figure it out himself for the first time. I was there to answer any questions, but he was the one who emailed the county and the state, and he was the one filing the paperwork. If you've ever done it yourself, you understand what an achievement that was for a 21-year-old.

Now, some of you may be saying, "A spending plan doesn't work for me. I've tried it." Two of the biggest complaints I hear are this: "Budgeting is too restrictive" and "My income is inconsistent from month to month."

Let's tackle this first limiting belief. When I decided to create a spending plan, it did feel restrictive at first, but that's more because I had to think about something in a different way, and change can take some getting used to. But very quickly, I came to see my spending plan as *less* restrictive because it actually gave me the power to allocate my money to wherever I wanted to spend it. It also showed me how much I was able to save every month and then put that money back into investments.

The second limiting belief is easier to challenge. If your income fluctuates from month to month, wouldn't it be wise to budget for some additional emergency savings for the leaner months? If you use your lower-earning months as a baseline, then even when you earn more, the spending plan still holds, and the extra can be allocated to savings or a separate pot for emergencies. I would feel a lot less stress about my ability to weather a few slow months of income knowing that I was being proactive in planning for them.

Now that you see the importance of a spending plan, let's walk through the process of making one. I'll start by saying that it is not nearly as complicated as it might sound! These are the steps you need to create a budget or spending plan:

1. List your income
2. List your expenses
3. Subtract expenses from income
4. Track your transactions as you make them
5. Make a new spending plan before the month begins (you can just copy the previous month)
6. Track all of your monthly expenses for the budget to work

While you are preparing your spending plan, I'll go over a few other money habits that worked extremely well for our family.

First, I created an emergency fund for any unexpected expenses that could pop up. With six kids, it seems like every month, there's a different emergency. Visits to the dentist, car issues, problems with the AC—any short-term, small unplanned bills or payments that aren't part of your routine monthly expenses. I kept $1,000 cash in an envelope for these unplanned expenses. As I used the emergency fund, I would replenish it.

The next step that I taught my children was to pay off all credit card debt monthly and to pay any mortgages and car payments monthly as well. I wanted to have as little personal debt as possible. Remember the free car for over eight years? I've been very fortunate in that I have never had a car payment in my entire life. I always paid cash for my cars and have chosen to buy pre-owned cars to save money as well.

While we are on the subject of credit cards, I'm not of the opinion that cutting up your cards and using only cash or debit cards is always best *unless* you can't control your spending and you've dug yourself into a deep financial hole. Hopefully, as you are reading this chapter, the habits you're learning and are going to incorporate into your life will help you avoid this reckless spending. When my children turn 18, I add them to my credit card account so they can start building credit. I can monitor what they spend on a weekly basis, and as they get older, I let them apply for their own cards.

My 18-year-old daughter just became a licensed massage therapist, so I told her to get a credit card for her business. She can use it for any business-related expenses, build credit, and easily track her expenses. When the bill comes due, she pays the amount off entirely. She also has a personal savings account, a checking account, and a business checking account.

You, as the parent, have to regularly check in with them about what's going on in their financial world. For my three oldest children, we have monthly meetings with our bookkeeper to go over their finances and update their business ledgers. When it's time to report sales tax or file their taxes, there should be very few surprises.

After you've established an emergency fund and taken control of your debt, I would establish another savings account with three to six months of expenses. You never know when disaster strikes. Or, what if you just want to quit your job and look for another one but have no way to leave because you have no money saved? Call this fund your Happy Savings Account.

Whether or not to go to college is another important subject that needs to be discussed as a family. There's no right or wrong answer here. I've changed my mind on this one, in fact. At first, I thought they all had to go. *I* went to college. How would it look if my kids didn't go? That's what I was thinking subconsciously.

But, once I understood and accepted that each child is unique, has their own gifts and talents, and should be able to decide for themselves whether or not they want to attend college, it was much easier to have the discussion. My first two children went to college, but my third decided to forego college and become a massage therapist. It's looking like my fourth child has zero interest in pursuing higher education at college as well, so they'll find another path.

How do you, as a parent, grapple with this immense decision? What helped me rationalize the cost of college was that I looked at it as a "Return on Investment." Could my child get a degree, not go into debt, and be marketable after they graduate?

I'm fortunate enough to be able to pay outright for my children to attend college. My mother paid for me when I went, and I want my kids to begin their adulthood with zero debt. This allowed them the flexibility to pursue their passion after graduating. My two oldest both decided to become missionaries after they graduated. In fact, as I'm writing this, my son is away this summer serving as a missionary. What an incredible experience for a young adult to be able to learn how to serve others and be in the service of the church.

There are a couple of things that a family can do to save on the costs of a college education. In Florida, there is a program called dual enrollment, where high school students take college courses while still earning their high school diploma. In fact, we have a lot of homeschool families whose children graduate high school with an associate's degree—a two-year college degree—for *free*.

Another way that I saved on college expenses was by having my children commute to college. I understand that many parents want their children to experience college life, but if having to take out debt for that experience is the only way, then I would pass on the experience and have them live at home to save.

The path to higher education has changed drastically since my generation. Nowadays, if a child is passionate about a subject, it can almost certainly be found online, or they can seek out a mentor.

Bottom line: you should view college as an investment in your child's future. Seek out a college that is very good academically yet will not saddle you with an inordinate amount of debt.

Before we end this chapter, I want to share with you Parkinson's Law of Spending, which is responsible for wreaking havoc on people's financial futures. It states that a person's expenses will increase in proportion to their income growth. In other words, any increase in income will be offset by an increase in spending.

Got a nice bonus at work? You opt to go splurge on a nice car. Land a promotion, and you decide that you deserve a bigger home.

I'm not here to judge. I was caught up in Parkinson's Law early on, and I can tell you by experience that trying to keep up with the Joneses produces a lot of unhappy money.

It isn't a new phenomenon, either. The phrase "keeping up with the Joneses" emerged in the 1950s as the U.S. entered a period of prosperity and innovation. It's been causing financial pain ever since.

How can you avoid being a casualty? Follow the steps we've laid out in this chapter. Awareness is the key to taking control of your financial future.

As we say in the Barbaro household, proper planning prevents poor performance.

Your Next Steps

1. Begin to involve your kids in money discussions.
2. Start playing games to teach them about money.
3. Create a spending plan (if you don't have one) and share it with the kids.
4. With your older children, begin the discussion of college and what their interests are.
5. Set up an emergency fund.
6. Keep personal debt to a minimum and pay off all bills monthly.
7. Save three to six months of living expenses.
8. *It's never too late to start!*

CHAPTER 4

BABY MONEY SOLDIERS

Beware of little expenses; a small leak will sink a great ship.
—Benjamin Franklin

It seems as if most people you speak to in the U.S. are living paycheck to paycheck. In fact, over 63 percent of the population lives this way, and half of them earn *over six figures*, according to *Forbes*. To make matters worse, only 5 percent of the population will be able to retire financially free. How can you explain the terrible financial situation that most people find themselves in?

It's because they haven't learned the concept of the Baby Money Soldier®, or BMS. In essence, BMS is the income that we earn throughout our lives, and we deploy it in various ways.

Let's start by discussing different kinds of income.

The Three Types of Income

1. **Earned:** Money that is "earned" from a job. It includes wages, salaries, tips, and commissions.

2. **Portfolio:** Money that is earned from interest, dividends, and capital gains on investments.
3. **Passive:** Income that is derived from rental properties, royalties, and limited partnerships.

The goal of living an abundant life and achieving financial freedom is to learn how to take your earned BMS and convert them into portfolio and passive BMS. You want your BMS to have more babies, not spend them on luxuries and kill your BMS. Your passive and portfolio BMS should be paying for your luxuries so that your overall BMS will continue to expand.

Before we dive into the various ways that you can deploy BMS, I'd like to share my thoughts on money and happiness with you. Money's intrinsic value is its ability to give you *control over your time*. What Jake and I discovered after thousands of hours of coaching students is that the vast majority of them are seeking time freedom. They want to be able to do what they want, when they want it or, just as important, with whomever they want.

The accumulation of money and the achievement of financial freedom grants you the ability to use your time however you choose. Happiness is achieved in most instances once we have autonomy over our time. Do you *want* to continue working? Can you tell your boss to fly a kite? Can you skip out of work and go watch your kid's soccer game?

When I left my restaurant back in 2016 and relocated to Florida, I actually had the opportunity to retire and sit on the beach. Instead, I chose to continue investing in multifamily real estate and launch our educational company, Jake & Gino. I made those decisions because I finally felt as if I had found my soul's purpose in life. What an indescribable feeling it is to be excited when Monday morning rolls around, and I have the opportunity to impact the lives of our members. It finally dawned on me that financial freedom was not about how much money you accumulate but the options that money provides for you and your family.

The quality of your life is in direct proportion to the quality of your decisions, and when you're able to make empowering decisions, your life will only improve.

Now, let's dive into the different ways we can deploy our BMS. Remember, every dollar that you earn from your job, a side hustle, or a passive investment is in your control to wield.

The Four Types of Expenses

1. **Variable:** Vary from month to month. Examples are *groceries, gas,* and *clothing.*
2. **Fixed:** Fixed month to month. Examples include *rent, insurance,* and *cable bills.*
3. **Intermittent:** Occur at various times in large sums. Examples include *car repairs, insurance bills,* and *college tuition.*
4. **Discretionary:** Non-essential things that we don't need. There is a huge difference between a need and a want. Examples include *eating out, vacations,* and *gifts.*

Let's begin with living expenses. At Jake & Gino, we like to say the three basic human needs are food, clothing, and apartments (a place to live). We all need to spend our precious BMS on other essentials, too, such as insurance and transportation. We have to learn how to limit our living expenses in the beginning because once the money is spent on these living expenses, your BMS will perish. There is no chance for it to multiply. These types of expenses can be categorized as living expenses.

This leaves us with discretionary expenses, which we will call luxuries, such as vacations, cars, jewelry, second homes, and designer clothing. The list goes on and on with luxuries.

Note—Some luxuries can be converted to creating more BMS. Your vacation home can be listed on Airbnb to generate more BMS, and your luxury car can be listed on Turo to rent to others, creating more BMS while you still enjoy this luxury.

Once we have established our living expenses, gotten our luxury expenditures under control, and allocated BMS to savings, it's time to unleash our Baby Money Soldiers and start taking over assets. I want you to picture the game of Risk, where the goal is to conquer new territories. That's the same mindset you want with your BMS that are allocated to investing. Their job is to focus on investing in an asset that is going to produce a yield (more BMS). Remember, you still have BMS in reserve for saving and spending.

As your BMS continue to conquer more assets, you will begin to witness what we call the snowball effect. Your assets will generate more BMS, and the goal is to redeploy these BMS to buy more assets, which will create more BMS. Where we see people fail in their financial plans is that they kill these BMS by buying luxuries and increasing their expenses rather than allowing the BMS to flourish. They, in effect, take them off the battlefield, thus squandering their resources.

Once you begin to accumulate more BMS, it's time to consider planning for your future and your legacy. Creating an estate plan is essential for the survival of your BMS and for having them pass on to the next generation. Did you know that over 65 percent of the people in the U.S. don't have an estate plan? People are allowing their BMS to be taxed again with the death tax, leaving even less BMS to pass onto their families. As you continue to expand your BMS army, it's vital to look to protect what you have built and what you will be building in the future.

As you continue to expand your assets, the utilization of **business debt** is essential to expanding your army. Where can you find more BMS? One place to find BMS is a lending institution, but it will cost you. We like to use the analogy of a mercenary, where you pay them to fight your wars.

The use of mercenaries to fight wars goes back as far as 2500 BC, and it allowed countries to field a larger force on the battlefield. When Jake and I purchased our very first multifamily property, we went to a bank and borrowed 80 percent of the proceeds for the purchase. Another 10 percent of the down payment was provided by the seller in the form of a seller carryback. Think about that for a second: 90 percent of the money we needed for the investment wasn't coming from us, even though we controlled 100 percent of the property. What an amazing way to hold back some of your BMS and deploy them elsewhere.

We view the money from the bank as our personal mercenaries, where we're paying the bank for the use of their BMS in return for us buying the asset. Mercenaries can be used to expand your BMS, such as buying cash-flowing real estate, or they can be used to deplete your BMS, such as buying luxuries.

Now, let's talk about spending our BMS on education. Jake and I have spent hundreds of thousands of dollars on our education and personal development, with the sole purpose of achieving an ROI (return on investment) from the education. When we decided to invest in coaching to scale up our companies, we set expectations and goals for the money we invested in our education. We expect the BMS we invest in ourselves to continue to fuel our growth.

When assessing whether you should attend college or have your children attend, what is the ROI? Are they going to become a lawyer or doctor, and is it necessary to attend? Or are they going to spend $200,000 on a useless degree only to decide they want to work at Starbucks? Skip college, save the BMS, and go straight to Starbucks.

Finally, BMS can be donated to your favorite charity to create an impact in others' lives. What's the point of working hard and accumulating wealth if you can't help those less fortunate than yourself? You may be depleting your army of BMS, but the cause is well worth it in the long run. It may be difficult for you to devote BMS while you are building your empire, but there are other ways to be charitable, such as donating your time or your expertise to others.

Let's recap the different ways to use BMS:

1. Expenses
2. Luxuries
3. Saving
4. Investing
5. Legacy planning
6. Protection
7. Borrow to invest more (mercenary)
8. Education
9. Charity

Deployment of Your Baby Money Soldiers

I want you to picture yourself as the general of your Baby Money Soldier army. You have to learn how to survey your financial battlefield and how to deploy your Baby Money Soldiers to expand and conquer more territory. That means, at certain times, it's an all-out attack (buying an asset). At other times, you need to withdraw some of your forces and redeploy them (sell an asset).

Some Baby Money Soldiers need to be deployed to protect the flanks of your army (asset protection and entity creation), while others need to be used to expand your supply lines (personal development). At times, you will need to hire mercenaries (borrow capital) to expand your footprint on the battlefield. Also, you have to make the decision every week how many Baby Money Soldiers are going to be sacrificed to pay for your living expenses and your luxuries.

As the general, you've got to make difficult decisions with limited resources to expand your BMS army. But when you start taking control of your resources and allocate them responsibly to accomplish specific tasks, you will be on your way to financial independence.

Now that you understand the different ways to use BMS, let's return to the concepts of poor, middle-class, and wealthy mindsets to explore how these mindsets use their BMS.

Rules of Thumb for BMS

1. Save 10 percent toward your Financial Freedom Account
2. Spend 60 percent on necessities
3. Spend 10 percent on luxuries
4. Save 10 percent for charity
5. Save 10 percent for education

Make sure you keep the following in mind:

- Your Financial Freedom Account is for investing only in assets.
- Necessities include living expenses such as rent, mortgage, transportation, and food.
- Luxuries include vacations, jewelry, and anything not deemed necessities.
- Education includes books, courses, seminars, and any material that leads to personal growth.
- Charity is the voluntary giving of help to those in need.

I would like for you to ponder this question: "Is your money working hard for you, or are you working hard for your money?"

It goes without saying that you need to work hard for your money when you begin your career. Unfortunately, I was stuck working hard for years without ever understanding how my money could work hard for me. Once I started having my BMS work hard for me, my financial picture began to change dramatically.

Now, it's time to teach you strategies on how to expand and protect your BMS. The first strategy to expand your BMS is to invest in assets that produce cash flow that creates more BMS. Jake and I have witnessed the power of investing in multifamily real estate, but there are countless assets to invest in to expand your BMS.

The next strategy to expand your BMS is to create a side hustle. When I was working at my restaurant, I decided to invest in real estate. All I was trying to do was to supplement my income to the point where I could leave my restaurant and become a full-time investor. Side hustles can include:

- Another job (Uber, commissioned salesperson)
- Consultant
- Amazon stores
- Vacation rentals
- Turo (renting cars)
- Short-term stock trading
- Fixing and flipping homes
- Buying a business

The options are endless! We interviewed Ryan Pineda, a social media influencer, on the Jake & Gino Show, and one of his first side hustles was flipping used couches. Let me say that again. He was *flipping used couches* and built the business up to generate thousands of dollars a month.

Another strategy to expand your BMS is to refinance one of your existing real estate deals. A refi and roll, as we like to call it, is the process of replacing your existing debt on a property with a new mortgage. The roll part is key in this process. We roll the proceeds from the remortgage right into a new asset. Hence, refi and roll!

Let me share an example of the process. On our very first deal, we paid $600,000 for a 25-unit apartment complex. We were able to secure seller financing, a strategy where the seller or owner of a property will finance the deal for you, just like a bank or traditional lender. The bank was financing 80 percent of the deal, and the seller was holding 10 percent of the down payment as a mortgage, meaning we only needed to come up with the remaining 10 percent of the money to close the deal.

The numbers looked like this. The mortgage from the bank was $480,000, the seller-financed note was $60,000, and the money we needed to close was $83,000 ($60,000 plus $23,000 in closing costs). As I stated earlier, we had two forms of mercenaries in this deal: the loan from the bank and the seller-financed note. In effect, we controlled a $600,000 asset with only $83,000 BMS out of our pocket.

We were able to increase the value of the property to over $800,000 over the next two years, and at that point, we went back to the bank to refinance a portion of the value created. We received a new loan from the bank for $650,000, replacing the old loan. That allowed us to extract an additional $165,000 BMS from the deal, and we still kept the seller-financed note with the sellers.

Let me recap what happened with this deal once we refinanced it. The loan was refinanced at a lower rate with a longer amortization period. Even though we added almost $200,000 to the original loan, our payment was basically the same. Our income had shot up during this time, which made our cash flow increase tremendously. We also performed a cost segregation study, which is essentially a study that allowed us to depreciate the asset much quicker, which helped us save a ton on our taxes.

This deal expanded our BMS on multiple fronts. We were able to save money on our taxes, we increased our cash flow monthly, and we refinanced a ton of BMS out of the deal. The *roll* part of refi and roll is critical. We didn't take the $165,000 BMS and buy luxuries. We invested them into our next deal, creating more BMS.

To this day, we still own this deal. It's cash flowing handsomely, it's continuing to appreciate, and we still have the mercenaries in the form of the bank loan and the seller-financed note. The owners love the seller-financed note because, to them, it's a form of receiving BMS every month from us.

We've been able to refinance and roll over $25 million BMS from our portfolio over the years, and it's been one of the most powerful strategies for expanding our assets and creating more BMS.

The next strategy is a 1031 exchange. A 1031 exchange, which gets its name from Section 1031 of the Internal Revenue Service Tax Code, allows investors to substitute one investment property for another and defer capital gains that they otherwise would have to pay when they sold the property. There are numerous rules and regulations to the exchange, but it's an amazing strategy for investors to preserve their capital and roll it into the next deal.

Years ago, when my family bought the restaurant, my mother purchased the building by using a 1031 exchange. She sold an investment property and rolled the proceeds into purchasing the building. She was able to defer hundreds of thousands of dollars of BMS and invest in the restaurant property by using the 1031 exchange.

Now, on to protecting your BMS. The first tool that we use to protect our BMS is the entity structure. We create limited liability companies (LLCs) and use them to hold our properties for liability protection. The LLC exists as a separate entity from us, and we can't typically be held personally responsible for its debts and liabilities.

Each one of our businesses is held in a separate LLC, and they each have their own operating agreement, a key document used by LLCs to outline the business's financial and functional decisions, including rules, regulations, and provisions. The purpose of the document is to govern the internal operations of the business in a way that suits the specific needs of the business owners, called "members." (Thanks, Wikipedia). The operating agreement is critical because it outlines the ownership and expectations of the members.

The next tool to protect your BMS may seem obvious, but most people underappreciate the value that it provides. This sexy tool is insurance. Okay, it's not sexy, but as we like to say, it's the moat that protects your castle. You go through life hoping you don't need insurance, but when the opportunity arises, how quickly you forget the premiums that you have paid up to that point.

Different Types of Insurance

- Renter's insurance
- Homeowner's insurance
- Auto insurance
- Umbrella liability insurance
- Life insurance
- Health insurance
- Disability insurance
- Long-term care insurance

When I owned the restaurant, we had a small fire in the kitchen. At least, I thought it was a small fire. As I stood on the roof with a garden hose trying to extinguish the flames spewing from the exhaust hood, all I thought about was, "How am I going to pay my bills and recover?" Not such a good idea to try to put out a grease fire with water, but a person will do almost anything when they see their future literally going up in flames.

I was blessed to have an amazing insurance broker who made sure we had the proper coverage, and the insurance company paid for the rehab of the building, the updating of the building to the current building code, the lost wages to all my employees, and our lost profits during the 11-week time period that we were closed. I can't recall what my yearly premiums were, but I'll never forget the $320,000 that I received from the insurance company.

Please take the time to review your line of defense with all of your insurance coverages. Some of these types of insurance may not be relevant to you at this point in your life. Just make sure to review your coverages yearly and adjust accordingly as your net worth increases.

Life insurance is an interesting type of insurance. Most people, especially those with poor and middle-class mindsets, view life insurance as an expense and purchase term life insurance due to its low cost. Jake and I have interviewed dozens of eight-figure net-worth individuals (net worth greater than $10 million), and every single one of them owns whole life insurance. They view it as an asset, and instead of "renting" term for a specified period of time, they want to own the whole life for the long term.

What better way to have some of your BMS in reserve than in a whole life policy, just waiting to be extracted for an opportunity? Whole life provides so many benefits, including:

- Safety
- Liquidity
- Leverage
- Guarantee
- Privacy
- Protection
- Tax advantages

Another strategy to protect your BMS and leave a legacy for your family is to create an estate plan and utilize trusts. I already mentioned that over 65 percent of the population does not have an estate plan. I was one of those people until I understood the power of BMS and creating a legacy for my family.

If you haven't begun the process, take baby steps. Create a will, and if you have children, establish a guardian in the event something happens to you and your spouse, then begin the conversation with an estate attorney about utilizing trusts to protect your assets from entering into probate once you pass away.

In my opinion, the goals of estate planning are to save your estate from onerous taxes, control what happens to your estate once you pass on, and—most importantly—limit the amount of fighting among family members. Let's face it: There will always be fighting, but how much? You can decrease the stress and chaos by planning now what happens when you inevitably pass on. Also, I want to leave a legacy to my kids and grandkids and teach them the power of financial education.

Finally, I want to share with you how to protect and expand your BMS. Essentially, it comes down to following six simple rules for you to dominate the BMS game.

1. Save BMS to invest in an asset.

In *The Psychology of Money*, author Morgan Housel makes a simple yet profound statement about creating wealth: The first idea—simple, but easy to overlook—is that building wealth has little to do with your income or investment returns but lots to do with your savings rate.

I agree wholeheartedly, but would add another caveat: the aim is for you to save money to buy an *asset* to pay for an event, not save money for the event itself. For example, we've been conditioned to save for retirement, save for kids' college funds, and the list goes on and on.

The deal Jake and I made for our first 25-unit apartment complex is still paying for my kids' college tuition. My oldest two children have both graduated. If I had taken the money I invested into this deal and saved it in a 529 plan, the money would have been barely enough to cover my first child's tuition, and then it would've been gone. No more, no mas, nada!

Instead, I still own the asset, the cash flow BMS are going to pay for my remaining four children, and when they've all graduated, I will still own this asset, printing BMS every month while the residents continue to pay down my mortgage and the asset continues to appreciate.

Become a diligent saver, and focus your savings on purchasing assets that will pay for your future events. The percentage of your income is up to you, but a minimum of 10 percent of your income is where you should start. As your BMS continue to grow monthly and your expenses remain stable, that figure should continue to increase.

As of this writing, Jake and I are able to save over 75 percent of our income each month to invest in more assets.

2. Control your expenditures of BMS, especially those deployed to luxuries.

This may be the most difficult rule to follow for most because of the ease of purchasing online and the ability of social media to continually remind us of how much our lives suck and how we have to keep up with the Joneses. But c'mon, who cares what the Joneses are doing? They're probably broke, with thousands of dollars of credit card debt and no clear path to creating any form of wealth.

We all need to be able to reward ourselves for our hard work and achievements, but getting caught in this vicious cycle will stop you from creating BMS. My recommendation would be to allocate a certain percentage of your earnings to savings and enjoy the rest. I will tell you that my ability to crush my instant gratification and wait until my assets could pay for my luxuries allowed me to become financially free much quicker.

3. Redeploy your BMS to conquer more territory.

This rule is pretty simple and straightforward, yet it could be called the most important one because this is the rule responsible for creating the cash flow snowball. Once you have money saved, go out and conquer more cash-flowing territories. Once Jake and I closed our first deal, we were able to close on our second deal three months later, and our third deal was closed six months after that. We were determined and disciplined to deploy our BMS to go out and invest in these assets.

4. Assemble BMS in reserve and avoid losing BMS in battle.

One of the biggest mistakes that investors and business owners make is that they invest all of their capital into the business or an investment. We've been taught by Wall Street and CNBC that the higher the risk, the higher the reward and every dollar needs to be put at risk to chase the highest yield. How did that work for people who followed this sage advice during the 2008 Great Recession and the 2020 Pandemic? Not so good!

On the one hand, the goal is to expand your BMS. On the other hand, what happens if you come up with unexpected liquidity issues or the economy decides to take a dive, as we are currently witnessing? Two things will occur. Number one, you may not be able to pay your obligations, and you will go out of business. The second scenario is that you will not have any capital in reserve to capitalize on the buying opportunities that will present themselves in the downturn.

We utilize our whole-life policies as a cash management tool for liquidity during the down times. Each one of our properties has what we call a capital expenditure account, where we save money monthly for those expected and unexpected expenses.

Finally, a word on investments that are showing a loss. Warren Buffet is famous for saying there are two rules in investing. Rule number one is "Never lose money." Rule number two is "Never forget rule number one." There comes a time in your investing career when you have to separate your ego from your investments and sell the investment at a loss if you think there is little hope of recovering any value to preserve your BMS.

5. Reinvest BMS in your education.

You are either growing or dying. Given the speed at which things are changing and evolving, if you do not continue to reinvest in yourself, you'll soon be dead in business. I want you to view spending money on your education as an investment, not an expense. Once you learn a skill, it will be yours forever. As Jake and I continued to evolve and grow, we have invested hundreds of thousands of dollars in coaches to scale our business, write books, host live events, train speakers, and so on. You are the most important asset, so continue to invest in yourself.

6. Only invest BMS with partners who share similar values.

I've learned this rule the hard way several times. When I didn't take the time to learn about my partners and their values and to see if their values aligned with mine, the partnership was doomed. My first investment, in a mobile home park, was a total disaster. I lost $172,000. That's a ton of BMS to lose! I will never forget that loss or the lessons I learned.

I could sit here and blame my partner, the investment, the market cycle, or my luck. But, once I adopted the wealthy mindset, I realized it was entirely my fault. If I had done due diligence on the investment or the partner, I would have never invested in the deal.

My plea to you is to invest with partners who share values and goals similar to yours. Jake and I are fully focused on multifamily and any business that is correlated to the asset. No shiny object syndrome, no crypto, and we buy deals for the long term. Our values and our mission are in alignment, and we enjoy speaking multiple times a day. If you can't have a beer with your partner, then you should rethink the partnership.

Let's recap the six rules to protect and expand your BMS:

1. Save BMS to invest in an asset.
2. Control your expenditures of BMS, especially those deployed to luxuries.
3. Redeploy your BMS to conquer more territory.

4. Assemble BMS in reserve and avoid losing BMS in battle (cut your losses).
5. Reinvest BMS in your education.
6. Only invest BMS with partners who share similar values.

CHAPTER 5

WEALTH BUILDING WITH PURPOSE

Long-term planning, patience, and collaboration to achieve a grand vision—that's Cathedral Thinking.
—Rick Sapio

Cathedral thinking is a mindset that leads to actions that don't immediately benefit *you* but that you know future generations will be able to enjoy. The term is derived from the cathedral builders of the Middle Ages, who most often knew that they wouldn't be alive to see their works completed but understood the importance of beginning their great work regardless.

When my wife and I had our first child, the discussion quickly turned to which school she was going to attend. I assumed, like most other normal people, that my daughter *would* be going to school. At the time, homeschooled families were viewed as weird, and their kids were assumed to have zero social skills and be less intelligent than kids who went to regular school.

Okay, that may be an exaggeration, but that's the way I felt. I had never met any homeschooled families before, and yet here was my wife, asking me to try it because her sister was doing it.

Did I embrace the idea? Nope. I remember feeling like an outsider every time a customer at my restaurant asked me where my kids went to school. I would sheepishly respond, "We homeschool them." It was even more embarrassing when a teacher, or in one case, the principal of the local high school, asked what school the kids went to.

There was even a group of contractors who would come into my restaurant for lunch once or twice a week, and I vividly remember how they would poke fun at me and the kids for homeschooling. I tolerated it, even though it wasn't always easy. I trusted my wife, but in the moment, I just had to have faith that we'd made the right decision.

As the years passed, I realized that homeschooling was one of the best decisions that we could have made for our family. My schedule at the restaurant had me working on the weekends, so I would have spent so much less time with my children if they hadn't been homeschooled. Instead, I was able to wake up in the morning and teach the kids for about 45 minutes before I went to work, which created a special bond between all of us. Plus, I still remember all 50 state capitals!

At this point, you may be asking, "Gino, what does this have to do with cathedral thinking?" *Everything*. That single decision to homeschool our kids altered the future of my family for generations to come. It put us on the path to meeting and becoming friends with some amazing families, it strengthened the bond among our children, and it gave our family the flexibility to control our own schedule. Not to mention, I think my wife would have gone mad if she had to be part of the Parent Teacher Association (PTA).

The decision also affected our children immensely. They've grown up in a household filled with love, faith, and a lot of kids. We instilled our values in them, and we were able to form close bonds with them. When you talk to my kids, they all want to have big families, and they all love each other. They're also independent thinkers, and their emotional intelligence is off the charts.

What I find to be funny and a bit ironic is that today, homeschooling is in vogue, and there's more support for and information about it out there than ever. It makes me happy that so many families have the courage to homeschool their kids and implement cathedral thinking, even though they may not be fully aware of the impact they're creating for future generations.

I may never get to meet some of my grandkids and great-grandkids, but the decision my wife and I made over 20 years ago has positively impacted future generations of Barbaros.

Take a moment to reflect upon this statement: **The decisions that you make today will affect not only your children but future generations as well.** When you understand and embrace the responsibility of that statement, you'll see that your actions and decisions should never be rash. Even when the choices you make are difficult and unpopular, you'll still make them because you realize how much is at stake.

This decision-making process allowed me to move from New York, a place where I had lived my entire life, to St. Augustine, Florida, back in 2017. If you're a New Yorker, then you can appreciate how difficult it is to leave. That's your identity, your mojo, your personality. But if I had remained, my kids would have found it difficult to buy a home and raise a family there due to high costs and high taxes. The state also was not in alignment with my values, so I made the decision to move.

Everyone thought I was crazy. Grandmothers were crying, customers were in disbelief, cousins were confused. We doubted ourselves many times, but the thought of altering our future for the positive was well worth the short-term pain of making a decision that was unpopular and difficult.

So, you see, the question is, how can you align wealth-building strategies with your family values and legacy goals? We need to focus on passing on our values and our philosophy. How do we do that? The way we use and pass on our money is a reflection of our values. Become acutely aware of how you spend your happy money.

I was taught as a young child to save money and not spend it. It took me years as an adult to understand the negative consequences of that scarcity mindset, and I'm still working through how I want to spend and pass my money on according to my values.

As you're planning your next investment, I'd like for you to look at that investment to see if it aligns with your values. For me, for example, I was attracted to real estate because it's a great fit for my values. It's a long-term investment, a wealth builder, slow and steady, and it can be transferred to the next generation. I also have much more control over my investment than if I had invested in Apple stock.

Plus, I enjoy real estate. One of the things that I liked most about my restaurant days was the customers and being able to employ people who could provide for their families. Once I started to invest with Jake, the similarities were apparent to me. We're not only serving our tenants, but we're also building an enduring property management organization to serve our investments *and* our employees as well.

I want to pass on the skills of investing to my children and help them build their own enduring organizations. Through real estate and the Jake & Gino community, I intend to pass on my values to my kids. In a later chapter, I'll touch on how I let my children participate in my real estate deals and how the educational community is a great way to pass on knowledge and values to my kids.

I don't want to become one of the families that fall victim to the Scottish proverb "Shirtsleeves to shirtsleeves in three generations." The first generation earns it, the second generation grows it, and the third generation blows it. History shows that over 70 percent of wealth is lost by the second generation, and over 90 percent is lost by the third generation.

My parents were the first generation. They were both Italian immigrants who embodied their own cathedral thinking. They both came here penniless and, with hard work and dedication, gave me and my brother a great upbringing and an amazing head start for us to continue to build wealth. The thought of squandering what my father sacrificed for us is one of the reasons why legacy is so important to me. His values of integrity, hard work, and family were instilled in me, and I'm passing on those values to my children. Where can you start? In Chapter Eight, I will be diving into estate planning and planning a legacy.

What Would the Rockefellers Do?, a book written by Garrett B. Gunderson, had a profound impact on the way I viewed legacy and how to plan a legacy for my family. The book's main theme is how wealthy families achieved their wealth and have been able to not only maintain the wealth but perpetuate it.

One of the ways to pass on your philosophy and your values is to create a Statement of Purpose or a Vision Statement. This statement expresses your vision, your values, and the legacy that you want to bestow to your heirs.

I review my Vision Statement yearly and continue to update it. I'll share parts of my Vision Statement here for you to get an idea of what mine looks like so that you can get a start on yours:

- Be a role model of family life for future generations. Be humble, ask for God's grace, and always work hard.
- Work toward what your purpose is in life—what you were born to do.
- Use money as a tool, not to accumulate it, but to invest it and to use it as happy money.
- Spend less money than you make, and always make your decisions based on cathedral thinking.
- Be a 100-percent-responsibility junkie, and always accept responsibility.

- You can either make happy money or excuses, not both.
- Decisions should be based on your values.
- Always look to be of service in other people's lives and adopt the service mindset.
- Live a life of abundance, not scarcity.
- Embrace Education × Action = Results.
- Profit is the fuel, not the destination.
- Adopt a growth mindset, one that's always willing to accept responsibility and learn.
- Don't be afraid to make mistakes.
- Learn how to view problems as opportunities.

I can always look at my Vision Statement and know that it will keep me focused on what I'm trying to accomplish. I also highly recommend you share your Vision Statement with your family. They may have some insights or ideas that can enhance your statement.

I also include in my Vision Statement books that I want the kids to read. These include

- My books, of course!
- *The Richest Man in Babylon* by George S. Clason
- *Rich Dad Poor Dad* by Robert Kiyosaki
- *Think & Grow Rich* by Napoleon Hill
- *Mindset* by Carol Dweck
- *Atomic Habits* by James Clear

It seems as if when we discuss wealth and legacy, most of us point directly to money. Right now, I'd like to explore other forms of wealth, which, in my opinion, far supersede money and, in fact, will help you to attract happy money into your life.

When you get a moment to reflect back on your life, what are the memories that you cherish? Is it that raise in pay? Is it buying a car or maybe a vacation? What I remember most and what has left a huge impact on my life is the relationships that I have created and maintained through spending my money.

I can start with my parents. They gave me an amazing childhood and the security to know that if I needed help, they were only a phone call away. Do you know how powerful and important it is for children to know that they have support from their family? My mother told me that growing up in Italy, her family would have been considered poor by today's standards. They grew their own food, owned some property, and were able to afford basic necessities. But if they didn't have enough bread to eat, they could always go to a family member down the street for help.

It's such an amazing feeling to know that if you need help, you have somewhere to turn. That mindset has trickled down to me, and I hope to pass that down to my kids.

Take a look at the other relationships in your life. I would be remiss if I didn't acknowledge my wife and the impact she's had on my life. She not only changed my life but helped transform me into the man, father, and leader that I've become. I know she would say the same about my influence on her over the years.

I can't forget my business partner, Jake, with whom I have created a mini real estate empire. There is no way I would be where I am today without his hard work and dedication to our partnership.

I'm also happy to acknowledge all the employees that I've had over the years. We always tend to remember the challenging ones, but wow, I've had so many good ones that have made my life and business a lot easier.

Happy and healthy relationships will definitely attract happy money, and vice versa. The difficult customers, the ones who seem to suck the soul out of your life? Should you continue that relationship? All I can say for certain is that that customer will be creating unhappy money for you.

By far, the biggest benefit of establishing our educational company, Jake & Gino, is creating an amazing group of investors who are looking to improve their lives. I've formed relationships with our members that will last a lifetime. In addition, being able to interview mentors such as Robert Kiyosaki, T. Harv Eker, Carmine Gallo, and Michael Franzese, just to name a few, has brought so much joy to my life. I've found my calling in life by being a teacher and a mentor.

In the book that Jake and I authored, called *The Honey Bee*, the protagonist, Noah, is a disaffected pharmaceutical sales rep who's looking to quit his job and find another path in life. (Sounds a bit like Jake back in 2009.) Noah meets an older gentleman named Tom, who, unbeknownst to Noah, is a multimillionaire who has a passion for beekeeping.

Tom picks up Noah on the side of the road one day while he's trying to change his flat tire and brings him to his home, Tributary Acres. Noah is flabbergasted when he finds out this simple-looking beekeeper owns a vast estate. He comes to find out that Tom was an entrepreneur who learned how to create multiple streams of income and was able to live life on his terms, tending to his bees and his passion for mentorship.

Throughout the book, Noah returns to visit Tom to seek advice on how to become financially free. Tom teaches Noah invaluable lessons about life and creating wealth. Noah starts with one stream of revenue, which is renting out his basement on Airbnb. Eventually, he's able to quit his job and goes on to amass a large real estate portfolio. Soon, he's at the point where his business is on autopilot, but he's beginning to lose his passion. It's as if the money has no purpose.

As Noah struggles to find his why, Tom's last lesson to him is telling him to create streams of *purpose*. "Money isn't your reason. It only funds it." I'm not going to give away the ending, but as I read it again, it brought me to tears. I love Noah's journey from a selfish, arrogant salesman to a man of purpose who was able to impact so many lives with the happy money that he created.

Most people think that when they become wealthy, that'll be the time that they can give back and donate, but charity comes in many forms. Even when I was barely scraping by, I still went down to Harlem to cook for the neighborhood. The time and the relationships that were created then far surpassed any check that I would have been able to write at the time.

As you're building your empire, think about where you'd like to make a difference in the world. Is it an orphanage? Your church? Do you love animals? Want to spend time with people living in assisted care? Are you handy and can help build homes?

Don't lose sight of *why* you're making money. Remember, **profit is the fuel, not the destination**. If you adopt the mindset of creating streams of purpose, you'll live in a state of gratitude, which will fuel your happiness and your desire to serve others even more.

To recap, think about these things before moving forward:

1. Cathedral Thinking
2. Create a Vision Statement for yourself and your family
3. Focus on the different forms of wealth (relationships, your health)
4. Figure out what your Streams of Purpose are going to be

How can you give back, now and in the future, in ways that are meaningful to you?

PART 2
FOSTERING A HAPPY FAMILY

CHAPTER 6

THE ART OF COMMUNICATION AND FINANCIAL TRANSPARENCY

To effectively communicate, we must realize that we are all different in the way we perceive the world and use this understanding as a guide to our communication with others.
−Tony Robbins

When my son Michael was 15 years old, he asked me if he could buy an amp for his guitar. I asked him how much it would cost, and his response was a nonchalant "Oh, $1,500." He had saved up $5,000 in the bank and was prepared to use his money to buy the amp.

I asked him what was wrong with the other amps in his possession. He responded, "Nothing," but he wanted this new amp. The sound of this new amp was incredible, he said. He really *needed* it.

My response was that I could not allow him to spend 30 percent of his net worth on a purchase that he *didn't* need. At that time, he understood the concept of net worth, and my recommendation was to find one that was cheaper or sell his other ones and purchase the new one.

For the next few months, the battle was on. The request would come up in passing, but I still held firm. I told him that when I found a deal for him to invest in, he could take his money and invest in the deal. I explained to my 15-year-old what a fantastic bargain I was offering him. I was going to dilute *my* equity so that he could invest in one of my deals, and the money he made from the deal would be able to pay for his amp.

Try convincing a 15-year-old to wait to put off a purchase to-day, liquidate all of his holdings, and *possibly* be able to purchase his dream amp sometime in the future. Not an easy task! I felt as if it was my job, though, my responsibility as a parent to say no to the purchase and to teach my child about using his money more wisely.

Well, as luck would have it, Jake and I came across a 146-unit portfolio later that year. I had Michael transfer his $5,000 to me, and I gave him ownership in the deal. This part was a lot easier than I had expected, probably because Michael had constantly heard me talking about buying deals and refinancing the capital. His thoughts went to getting his $5,000 back in a couple of years and still having cash flow come in every month. The key to convincing him was be-ing transparent with him for all those years about how my real estate business worked.

The deal was an incredible bargain, which led us to refinance it within 18 months. We also sold two of the properties in that portfo-lio of 146 units. We were cash-flowing monthly from the portfolio, which I distributed to my son monthly.

What ended up happening was totally unexpected. He com-pletely forgot about buying the amp. Instead, when he got his $5,000 back (actually, it was a lot more than that), he decided to keep it in his savings to invest in our next deal.

Fast forward to today, and my son has invested in seven of our deals, with owner draws of over $3,000 per month (that's pure cash flow). His net worth is creeping toward $1 million, but that isn't the best news that's come out of his investing.

What could be better than that? The mindset that he's created over the past seven years is admirable, even for an adult. He saves his monthly draws and his equity distributions for the next deal. He's becoming a producer instead of a consumer, focusing on investing his money instead of buying something that he really doesn't need.

Last year, we closed on three deals. Before we closed the final deal in December, Michael had wanted to use some of his equity to buy a gun. I told him about the closing and needing capital, and his response was, "I can wait a few months to buy it."

Soon after his first investment, my other children became interested in investing alongside me. They saw their brother getting paid, and they wanted to know how they could participate. Now, my two oldest daughters are invested in several of my deals as well, and my third daughter is on deck waiting to invest her money.

Do you remember when I said your language becomes your experience? It's an amazing thing when you put skin in the game, and to Michael, his $5,000 represented a lot of skin. Every month, he would ask me how the deals were performing, and he was learning words such as economic occupancy, draws, op ex, cap ex, and refinance. He was learning the language of investing *and* real estate, and more importantly, he was learning the language of business.

One month, the portfolio didn't produce a draw—we weren't making money that month. He asked me why, then asked me another question that I didn't have the answer to. His question was, "How many units were renovated in the portfolio since we took it over?" I felt pretty dumb because I didn't have an answer for him. That led to our property management company creating a new system that tracked the number of units that needed to be renovated and made sure we were on schedule to renovate *all* the units eventually.

A renovated unit was much more desirable, had fewer expenses, and generated more income.

Michael just wanted to know why he wasn't getting paid, but it made us come up with a solution to a problem we needed to take care of.

Our focus now was on turning the units (renovating them) and getting them leased to market rent. That one metric has since been incorporated into every deal we purchase since we started with this portfolio. What a game changer for our property takeovers and leasing staff! I can't tell you why we weren't tracking it before. Maybe it's because our portfolio was smaller and didn't need this type of detail. Whatever the answer, a 16-year-old boy was able to ask the right question because he understood the language.

He's also learned how to ask his dad for seller financing. He wants me to lend him money to invest in a deal while he pays me interest. He understands that ownership and equity are where the value lies, and taking on business debt to grow his business is a wise decision—if you know what you're doing.

I'm not sure there are many teenagers out there who know what seller financing is, let alone try to use it on their dads. I have to say, it was a proud moment for me to see how far he'd come in so short a time. Oh, by the way, the answer was unequivocally NO! I wanted to teach him that he needed to create value to obtain seller financing, and I wasn't receiving any value by giving him seller financing. He was receiving *all* the benefits.

You may be thinking, "I don't have any real estate to invest in." That's okay. Teaching your kids these principles can be achieved by using various vehicles. It can be as simple as showing your child the interest they are earning on their savings account. You could open up a trading account at a brokerage firm and start to invest in stocks. Mutual funds are a great way to indoctrinate your children into the world of investing, too. Whatever investments you're making, be sure to include your kids and let them hear you talk about it.

I've recently taken my son's relationship with money to another level. When Michael turned 21, I felt he was ready to join Dave Ramsey's Financial Coach Program. I'd like for my son to build financial and coaching skills to help other young adults who are struggling with money or are financially illiterate. I want him to continue to adopt the service mindset and to help his peers in the realm of finance.

The conversations that have sprung from watching the lessons he's learning are incredible. He believes in some of Dave's philosophies on money, but he looks at debt through a different lens. I've taught him the difference between personal and business debt and how to leverage business debt to pay for personal expenses. He would never have been able to make that distinction if I wasn't communicating and sharing my journey of investing.

My goal throughout my children's journey with money has been to have them create a healthy relationship with money. At times, I failed miserably. But with grace, being able to learn from mentors, and constantly educating myself, I've learned from my mistakes and been able to share these mistakes with my kids.

I remember reading the *Wall Street Journal* with my dad when I was a kid. I fell in love with the stock market and would read the stock pages with him. He would share with me the stocks he was investing in, as well as the real estate buildings he was buying. My first job while in college was working at A.G. Edwards, a stock brokerage company, as a receptionist and support for the brokers. I caught the investing bug and continued to trade my own account in college. I ended up getting a degree in Finance, and my love for investing and making money continued to grow.

What are some of the skills or habits that I think we should be teaching our kids to succeed in today's world? Here are my top four:

- Needs versus wants
- Instant gratification

- Price versus value and the true cost in hours
- Listening

These are the skills that my son learned while he was investing with me. If we can teach our children the difference between a need and a want, then they can start making conscious decisions on what to buy.

I always try to bring in the lesson that life isn't fair. A *need* is anything that's required for human survival. Remember, we like to say at Jake & Gino that the three basic human needs are "food, clothing, and apartments." A *want* is something that people desire. We all have limited resources, and we need to prioritize our purchases based on what we need. Only then can we consider whether we can afford what we want.

In Michael's example, he *wanted* an amp—he didn't need one. I was conditioning him to begin to look at every purchase through that lens so that his decisions could be based less on emotion and dopamine and more on control and true need.

I was also conditioning him to try to delay his gratification. We now live in a world where almost anything we need is readily available, and there's little thought of waiting for it. If I want the amp and I can't afford it, I'll just put it on the credit card and pay the bill for the next ten years. Let's fast forward this into adulthood, where Michael could be saying to himself, "I want this nice big house I can't afford, but I can take out this huge mortgage and be a slave to paying it for the next 30 years." This is the last thing that I want for my children, and because of what they've been exposed to, I'm confident that Michael will be much less likely to fall into this trap.

My goal is to teach the kids to try to take the impulsiveness out of purchases. Once the emotion wears off, you can make a much wiser decision as to whether you really want it and can afford it. Studies have shown that kids who can delay gratification grow up to exhibit more self-control. They also understood that important things won't come easy in life. They take work and dedication, two traits that are destroyed by instant gratification.

Finally, you'll find it almost impossible to create sustaining wealth if you have the instant gratification bug. You will always find something to spend your savings on, leaving you with nothing to invest.

The third skill that I want you to teach your child is price versus value. Warren Buffet is famous for saying, "Price is what you pay, value is what you get." First, a child needs to understand what something costs. My example to my children is this: "If you are making $10 an hour at your job, and it costs $500 for the TV, then it just cost you 50 hours of work to buy that TV. Is it worth it to you?" Once you put it in those terms, they can understand the cost in a very personal way. Some may say, "Yes, I need it." Some may say, "I have to look for a cheaper TV." And some may say, "The heck with that. I'll skip the TV and buy something else."

This is where happy money comes into play. If an activity or object brings you immense joy, then you'll value it more highly. If it costs you $2,000 to go on vacation to Italy, where you've always wanted to go and sip espresso sitting on the Amalfi Coast, the cost may be great, but the experience and value are far greater than the price of the trip. My goal with all of these habits I'm teaching my children is for them to be able to make informed decisions and to focus on happy money.

There are two tools that I learned when I went to life coaching school that have transformed how I communicate with others. My wife, who was a huge doubter of life coaching early on until she saw the results that I was achieving coaching Jake & Gino members, decided to become certified. She's become a master of these two skills:

- Listening
- Asking empowering questions

God gave us two ears and one mouth, and we should use them in that proportion. You should be listening around 80 percent of the time and talking around 20 percent. Most people think that if they're not speaking, then they aren't communicating. But in reality, the person who is listening and asking questions is the one who's controlling and directing the conversation.

Are you the type of person who, while you're trying to listen, is getting ready to fire off your next thought? You're not listening if you're that guy (or girl). One of my mentors once told me, "To be interesting, you need to be interested." It took me a while to understand what he meant, but as I began to learn how much people love to hear themselves talk, I also saw how you can make someone feel important and special if you just give them the chance to express themselves. You'll become the cool kid on the block!

Your children want to be heard. They want, deserve, and need your full and undivided attention. You need to master the skill of listening by becoming more patient and curious about others. It's truly amazing what you can learn from others if you ask the right questions.

This brings us to our next skill: asking empowering questions. These are thought-provoking, open-ended, challenging questions that allow a person to take the time to reflect and search within themselves for an answer. An empowering question has to start with "What," "How," or "Who," and more importantly, you are not aiming for a yes/no answer. An example of a close-ended question would be, "Are you scared about going to school?" A better question would be, "What would make you scared about going to school?

You can also use the word "why," but be careful. It may sometimes come off as being judgmental.

When you ask your kids, "How was school?" you probably get the same response every day: "Good." Instead, ask, "What was the one thing you enjoyed about school today?" They're forced to share a lot more info, which will lead to you asking more questions. Tony Robbins is famous for saying, "Successful people ask better questions and, as a result, they get better answers." I'd like to say successful parents ask better questions, and as a result, get better answers and better connections with their kids.

One phrase that has stuck with me since I graduated from life coaching school is this: "What people say is about them. What you hear is about you." I always wondered why two people could have wildly different reactions to a situation. For instance, if one person sees someone driving a fancy sports car, their reaction may be, "Wow, that's cool. I want one." That's how I react when I see one. I know the hard work that it takes to afford one. But someone else may react differently and think, "What a show-off, and what a waste of money."

It comes back to your relationship with money and the filters through which you're viewing the situation. Are you viewing money as evil or as a tool to enjoy?

Let's go back to the quote. In this situation, what a person says about the fancy car reveals a lot about themselves. Just as importantly, the person receiving the information hears it through *their* filters. If that person has high self-esteem and is sure of themselves, the comments won't affect them. But, if the person is having a difficult day and is always out to prove their worth, the comment will be perceived very differently.

The great Steven Covey, author of *The 7 Habits of Highly Effective People*, discusses the stimulus-response model in his book. When you have a conversation with your kids, for example, you will have a response. The space between the stimulus and the response is where we're free to choose *how* we respond. You hear the word "trigger" being thrown around today. It's your choice if you want to be triggered or not.

Let me repeat that. *You* have the choice to be offended by a comment because what you hear is about you.

Once you understand you have the power to formulate your response to being stimulated, the world changes. You have control of your own thoughts and actions!

I'd like to share a story of how I failed miserably in stimulus-response. I came home one day from work to see one of my daughters making meatballs. It had been a stressful day for me, but I felt it was my duty to help her make the meatballs. After all, I was the meatball king. I personally cooked over 100,000 meatballs when I owned the restaurant. That's a lot of meatballs in an over 20-year career!

I perceived that my daughter should have been using a bigger bowl to mix the meat, the meatballs were too big, and she wasn't using an ice cream scooper to shape them. I proceeded to take over, and she pushed back, saying she didn't need my help. I felt as if I was triggered by my daughter, and I exploded on her, screaming at her and embarrassing myself. I had no right to act that way, and I shouldn't have even offered to help her. Looking back at the situation, she clearly didn't need my interference, and she didn't ask for it.

What people say is about them. My daughter was right in saying she didn't need help. She'd prepared meatballs countless times. What I heard or perceived her saying was that "You don't know what you're doing. You're doing it wrong. You need my help."

Those were my faulty filters. If I had just paused and understood the state I was in, my reaction would have been totally different. I would have allowed her to continue on her own, and if she did need help, she would have come and asked. I initially blamed my reaction on her. She "triggered" me when in reality, I was the moron at fault.

Thankfully, after several hours, I was able to apologize to her, but every time I think of that story, I'm so embarrassed by how I reacted. I should have known better, but I allowed my emotions to control my actions.

Take a moment to pause and reflect on if that's ever happened to you. If it has, now may be the time to reach out and say sorry.

One thing that I've learned to do over the years is to say sorry to my kids. This is a tough one for me. Saying sorry means admitting wrongdoing, and when you're raised in a family where you're accused of doing wrong things frequently, it can be challenging to change your thinking around that. Please learn how to say sorry to your kids, though, especially if you're at fault. If I'd decided to harbor that anger with my daughter, our relationship would be very different. Your kids need to see that you are fallible and can accept responsibility for your actions. This will help them learn how to accept responsibility for *their* actions as they get older.

When the trust is high with your children, communication becomes easier, and you will be the first person they come to for advice or help—not their friends or, even worse, the internet.

Your next steps:

- Start conversations with your kids, and share your financial picture with them.
- Pick an investing vehicle that you can teach them.
- As your kids get older, create monthly meetings to go over your financials (credit cards, budget, savings, investments).
- If your kids decide to start businesses, create monthly meetings with a bookkeeper to go over financials—and be on those meetings with them!
- Become a better listener and learn how to use empowering questions.
- Say sorry when you are wrong!

CHAPTER 7

SHARED DREAMS: ALIGNING FAMILY ASPIRATIONS

Coming together is the beginning. Keeping together is progress.
Working together is success.
–Henry Ford

It had been a tough day at the restaurant. As I entered the laundry room smelling like garlic and feeling like a wet rag from sweating all day, I approached my wife and asked her an almost impossible question. "Julia, what do you think if we sell the restaurant and I go into real estate full-time?"

She stood there for a few seconds, which felt like an eternity to me, and then she responded, "If that's what you need, then let's do it and we'll figure it out."

That's all I needed to hear. Ever since my father passed away, I had been moving farther and farther from wanting to work there.

Deep down, I felt that something was off. I was working at a job that was creating unhappy money, but, at the time, I didn't fully understand why. Looking back, though, it's obvious what was causing the pain. I was working somewhere that didn't align with my values. I value family, personal growth, and responsibility, and these values were slowly eroding as I continued to work there. I realized that I was created for more: that God gave me gifts, amazing parents, and an opportunity to achieve my dreams, yet I was "hiding" in the kitchen, washing dishes and sweeping the floor.

The choice I faced at that moment was this: Should I continue along a path that creates very little happiness for me but feels comfortable, or should I go and seek my soul's purpose that I was created for?

My wife had every right to question my decision and even to make the excuse that now wasn't the right time. She could have responded with, "Honey, we can't risk the money we've saved. The restaurant is safe and steady, and you want to risk all of that for real estate?" But she witnessed the pain that I was experiencing—the unhappiness, the fear of an uncertain future, and my feelings of an inability to provide for the family—and she didn't want that to continue. Instead, she was fully supportive of us diverting from our current road and taking one far less traveled.

With that single yes, a huge burden of responsibility fell upon my shoulders. If you are going to ask your spouse to radically upend your family's life, you'd better be fully committed. My wife had total confidence in my ability to pursue this new endeavor. She had seen me work countless hours over the past couple of years to become a more educated and experienced investor. I stopped wasting time on the TV at home, and even on my days at the restaurant, during every break, I was working on the real estate business.

I often got comments from people asking me why I was working so hard. I would work on real estate before I left for the restaurant, over my lunch hour, and after we put the kids to bed. I wanted to show my wife that I was fully committed to the decision I made, a dedication that she deserved. She was counting on me to not let the family down.

In October of 2015, I decided to work during the week in real estate and go to work at the restaurant on the weekends. That lasted for six grueling months, and finally, in March of 2016, I "retired" from the restaurant and became a full-time real estate investor.

Communication among spouses and your children is the key to a happy family, as well as to aligning your goals and aspirations. If I hadn't shared my ongoing struggles with my wife and rather had decided one day to ask her about selling the restaurant out of the blue, I'm positive her response would have been completely different.

She still didn't fully understand why I wanted to leave the restaurant. It's amazing to look back and see that we never had a deep conversation about money. I kept telling her that I wanted to become financially independent, but in her mind, we already were. I was making enough money to support the family, and our basic needs were being met.

My hope for you and your family is that you sit down and have an honest conversation about money. Julia and I had radically different upbringings with regard to money. Her parents divorced when she was young, and her mom worked two jobs just to provide for the kids. My parents were both immigrants who grew up relatively poor in Italy. Their focus was to start a business, save money, and enjoy the middle-class lifestyle.

When we got married, I assumed we were on the same page when it came to money. We decided that she was going to stay home and raise the kids while I would provide financially. My wife was an amazing worker. In fact, we met at the restaurant, and she was a machine. She could wait on 15 tables, answer the phone, bus her tables, and run out the food from the kitchen all by herself. And because of that, she made great money in tips.

But I would find money all over the place—in her pockets, on the table, in the car. She wasn't used to planning and saving, while I was completely the opposite. When I told her I wanted to become financially independent with real estate, Julia didn't understand what I meant. It was my mistake because I hadn't explained to her before what my definition of financial independence was.

To me, it meant not having to stress about every dental procedure (man, braces for six kids adds up), having a future where I could take a vacation without worrying about the bill, and the ability to be more generous with my tidings. If I wanted to pay for one of my relative's vacations, then I could. Once she understood my perspective, it was so much easier to communicate my aspirations, and she agreed with my view of creating this happy money from real estate and understood my passion for pursuing it.

It took years for our communication to truly flourish, and that's where listening to your partner comes into play. I never really took the time to see things from her perspective and understand her upbringing, and early on, I didn't share with her my fears and frustrations.

After I "retired" from the restaurant, I was confronted with another hard reality. I was still living in New York, but I felt as if the state wasn't aligning with my personal values. I also needed more of a separation from the restaurant. My mom was still calling me up, wanting me to come in and lend a hand. I was torn. How can you say no to your mom?

So, I decided to ask my wife if we could move to Florida. That would have been unthinkable to me five years earlier—just picking up the family and moving to another state? Once again, she paused, but then she gave the okay. I knew what I was asking. To take my wife and kids away from our family and relocate to a place where we knew no one was a big deal. But Julia realized that I needed boundaries from my family, and I also wanted to leave New York. The cost of living was too high, and the taxes, the weather, the politics, none of it aligned with what I wanted.

My wife felt the same way. She even told me that if we didn't make it in Florida, we could always move back to New York and live in my mom's basement. When I heard that, I truly understood how committed she was and how I couldn't fail. There's *no way* I was going to let that happen.

Was it a difficult choice for us to uproot the kids and take them away from friends and family to a new place filled with uncertainty? It was one of the toughest decisions that we had to make. But we realized that *our* relationship and happiness came before the kids.

Now, let me explain before moms and dads start hyperventilating. It seems as if parents today place all the emphasis on their kids—their activities, their school, their friends—and neglect their own relationship. I think that the happiness and health of the parents should come first. There are obviously certain situations where a child has special needs, or a crisis occurs for a child, and that child's situation has to take priority. That's not what I'm talking about.

I often hear parents say that they have to wait until their kids graduate from school before they can relocate or look for another job. I've got news for you: the kids are going to leave someday. You and your spouse are going to be left alone, and I personally didn't want to live a life of regret because I used my kids as an excuse not to try new things in life because they were going to be uncomfortable in the short term.

If the parents are happy, that joy will spread to the kids. How do I know? When I was working at the restaurant, I would often come home grumpy and unhappy. The kids, along with my wife, experienced it, and it was unfair to them. I think parents should do what's in the best interest of their relationship and for the family. That includes making tough decisions that your kids may not agree with or even like.

Was it easy when we moved? I wish I could say a resounding "yes." I was living my best life, and my oldest two children adapted quickly. My wife found it challenging in the beginning to develop friendships, and she had to find a new homeschool group to join. She felt the loss of not having her family close by.

My oldest daughter started college in the town we moved to, and my son found it much easier to adapt as well. My second and third daughters were miserable for a couple of years but, with time, actually came to love living down here. Now, at times, I hear comments such as "I can't even imagine living up north right now." The two youngest children had very little trouble adjusting to their new surroundings.

Once again, communicating and listening to your spouse is crucial to creating a happy family environment. My wife understood why I needed to leave New York, and I understood that if it didn't work out, we were heading back. But our happiness and relationship were of paramount importance for our family to thrive in the long term.

We were also teaching our kids some invaluable lessons. First, they learned how to make a difficult decision with a spouse. Second, they learned how to have the flexibility to change a plan. Third, they experienced that pain and being uncomfortable in the short term can lead to a wonderful outcome. Nothing truly worth it in life comes without a price, and we did pay that price early on.

What are some things that *you* can do as a family to expand your happiness? I think families should try to do everything together. We were never convinced that driving all the kids to separate functions was a healthy thing for us. Instead, when one played a sport, they all played the same sport and on the same teams. In fact, three of my daughters are playing volleyball right now, and we're able to go and watch their games together.

If you're pushing the sports angle in the hopes of your child getting a scholarship someday, I have to tell you that the percent chance of your child becoming a professional athlete is incredibly low. One statistic showed that out of 156,000 male high school basketball players, only 44 were drafted to play in the NBA. That is a 0.03 percent chance of becoming a professional.

I grew up playing sports, and it was such an important part of my childhood, but it wasn't a detriment to the family. Mom wasn't driving around every weekend, taking me to the ball field and leaving my brother. We grew up playing the same sports together.

I understand that I'm probably going to get a lot of pushback from parents who feel the opposite, that trying to get a sports scholarship is important. I just think that the family together supersedes all else if you're trying to achieve a happy home life.

We have six children, so it would be *impossible* for us to have our kids in different activities. Julia would literally be a taxi service, and I would never see her. We would never get a chance to eat dinner together at night as a family, and our weekends would be consumed by the kids' activities.

What can you do together as a family? We decided to find activities that they could all enjoy. We began to take singing lessons together. When one child decided to take gymnastics, we enrolled two siblings. Art class is a lot more fun when four kids take it at once.

We've tried to keep our family life as simple as possible. We've never had any pets unless chickens count. I never wanted to be responsible for taking care of an animal and have our schedule revolve around a pet.

We always go on vacation as a family. The idea of a vacation to me is to literally "vacate" my current situation and go on a new adventure, and I always want the kids with us. We also tried to do other things together as a family. When COVID-19 hit, we decided to start watching one show together every night. It started with *Chuck*, followed by *Burn Notice* and *Monk*. It's our time as a family to wind down and sit together. We're currently watching *The Dead Zone*.

The job of parents is to prepare their child for the road, not the road for the child. The most difficult moments for me as a parent is to see my children struggling with something. My impulse is to help them out right away. I remember one time when my son Michael had just started college, and he was in an accounting class. The work, even to me, was challenging, to say the least. He came to me for help, and I told him that he should try to figure it out. He started to cry out of frustration, and I wanted to cry, too. Instead, I sat down with him and walked him through the lesson. I didn't give him any of the answers. I just let him know I was there, and he eventually worked through it himself.

To me, it was a defining moment for his maturity and his confidence. I could have sat there and fed him the answers, but that would have only weakened his confidence. I wanted to let him know it was *okay* if he didn't know the answers. Part of being an adult is trying to figure things out. We don't have all the answers right off the bat, and the sooner a child knows this, the quicker he will learn to explore to find those answers.

There was another time when my oldest daughter, Gabriella, was struggling with something. I don't even remember what it was exactly. I do remember standing there, silent and helpless, as she began to weep. All I did was hold her and comfort her. Sometimes, being held is all kids need. I knew I didn't have the answer, but all Gabriella really needed was for me to listen to her and let her know I loved her.

As parents, our instinct is often to immediately take away any burden or discomfort for our kids. In my opinion, though, our job is to create a safe, open, happy environment where kids can thrive and become adults who can make their own decisions about the life they want to lead, following the purpose that God created them for.

Now, I don't let my kids run wild with no structure. We expect our children to help with daily tasks around the house, including cooking, cleaning up after meals, and maintaining a semblance of tidiness in their rooms. If a special project is involved, then compensation will follow. I don't believe kids should get paid for being part of the household.

Admittedly, our situation may be a bit different from yours. Every meal entails cooking for eight people. That's 24 dishes, forks, and knives every day! If you want to eat, you need to pitch in.

Children need structure in their lives, and running a family is very similar to running a business. Employees and children need to be heard, complimented when the job is done well, understand what the job is, be reprimanded in private when they make a mistake, and have certain expectations. Whatever you focus on will grow and thrive, and your family is no different.

Every outstanding organization has core values, and I think families should, as well. These should be values they choose together, values they live by, and values they can look to when making a decision. In our household, mass on Sunday is a non-negotiable. We all go together, no excuses. When I'm traveling for the weekend on business, I need to find a church to go to on Sunday.

Sit down with your kids and spouse and begin to map out what your core values are. My friend and mentor Rick Sapio created the family placemat, where you can create rules and list out your family's values, goals, prayers, or whatever is important to your family. You can see a few examples at familyplacemat.com.

To us, mealtime is sacred and strengthens our family. It's the time of the day when every family should have a "tech fast." No devices, no TV, no distractions. The children will follow your lead. If you're listening to your phone beep and not being fully present, how can you expect them to?

As we work toward strengthening our relationship with our kids, there are a couple of things I wish I had done sooner:

1. Say sorry to them.
2. Listen to them, and be less eager to give advice.
3. Teach abundance.
4. Let them find their soul purpose. Don't live your life through them.

In addition, here are some actions you can take to begin to create a happy family!

Next steps:

1. Talk to your spouse about your goals.
2. Have a conversation about money with your family and your spouse.
3. Focus on the health of your relationship. You are on the same team!

PART 3

CRAFTING A HAPPY LEGACY

CHAPTER 8

RESILIENCE THROUGH FINANCIAL EDUCATION & LEGACY PLANNING

I don't care about the money. I care about the legacy.
    −George Steinbrenner

It was a warm, sunny day in August. We'd just gotten back from a week-long vacation at the Jersey Shore, and the entire family was at my mom's house. My father had been diagnosed with cancer in March of that year, and his disease had progressed rapidly, leaving him very sick.

My mother fully dedicated herself to my dad during the last few months of his life. She was by his side every day and took care of his every need. This day, though, was particularly sad. My parents' priest and their accountant were also at the house. Father Luke was there hearing my father's confession and performing the sacrament of last rites.

But why was the accountant there? Unfortunately, my parents had kept procrastinating about getting their estate in order. The accountant was talking to her about setting up an irrevocable trust, stepping up in basis (as in, adjusting the cost of an inherited asset to its fair market value on the date the owner died in order to save on capital gains taxes), and other estate planning tools to help prevent her from entering probate and save on estate taxes.

One of the assets in the plan was the restaurant we owned. The name of the entity that owned the restaurant was Barile, and it was named after my dad's town in Italy. Even after we sold the restaurant back in 2020, she continued to keep the trusts open. It was as if she was still holding onto my dad and his memory.

In 2023, I finally convinced her to get her estate plan in order before I was put in the same situation as she'd been almost 20 years ago. I now know why it was so hard for her to dissolve the entity and let it go, but I don't want you to make the same mistake.

I think it was hard for her to work on her estate plan because doing so brought up memories of that day back in August. My mother wasn't given the time to grieve my father's death properly. She was thrust into making difficult decisions while under massive duress. She was consumed with the uncertainty of her financial future on top of the reality of losing my dad, with whom she had built an amazing life.

Fortunately, our accountant and attorney are both terrific, and they helped her get her financial house in order. She also had two sons who were there to support her and help her with the finances.

You may be asking yourself, "Why are you sharing this story, and why is it important to me?" If you're ever in my mom's situation, like so many of us will be, someday, I want you to be able to grieve the loss of a loved one properly. I want you to make empowering decisions about your legacy when you're not under stress, when you can properly plan, and when you can share your future aspirations with your spouse and kids.

By planning your estate now, rather than leaving it too late, you can make sure things will happen the way you want:

1. Your assets are distributed how you want.
2. You can give someone else the authority to make decisions if you are unable.
3. Your beneficiaries are clearly defined.
4. You can avoid probate. You do not want your heirs to go in front of a judge and have to prove that they have a right to your property. It's expensive, time-consuming, and offers no privacy whatsoever.
5. An estate plan will keep your legacy organized.

The definition of estate planning is "the preparation of tasks that manage an individual's financial situation in the event of their incapacitation or death." I was told by my attorney that he looks at estate planning as a legal toolbox, with certain tools that can manage your affairs while living and when you pass away.

So, where do you start? One small step at a time.

What I'm about to share is not to be construed as legal advice. It's my personal journey navigating the estate planning process. One thing I've learned is that you are never done. Either your family will continue to grow, or you'll accumulate more assets, or your wishes and desires will change over time.

There are two things you need to do before you embark on this lifelong journey:

1. Hire a competent attorney who has experience with estate planning. **Please** skip downloading documents online and trying to do it yourself.
2. Review your plan at least annually with your spouse and children. If you have a plan but haven't looked at it in years, it's time to get it out and update it.

At the time I got married and had my first child, I was woefully unprepared. I had already accumulated some assets, and my family was starting to grow. I needed to do something to make sure they would be taken care of if the worst happened. I started by drafting a will, a legal document that allows individuals to direct the way their inheritance will be distributed in the event of passing away. I also had to make the agonizing decision to select a guardian for my daughter in the event of my wife and I both passing away. You don't want to leave it to the state to make the decision for you, let alone allow your child to end up in the foster system.

You can also choose a separate person, a financial guardian, to manage the assets of the estate. We chose one guardian for our children and another financial guardian to manage the estate. For me, it was important to spell out in the will at what age my children had access to money. I didn't want my 18-year-old to have access to ALL the money we'd saved for them right then and there. I was able to declare at what ages our kids would be receiving their share of the money. As I recall, I started at 25, then went to 30, and finally ended at 35. If you haven't taken this step, *do it now.*

This was also the time I decided to purchase life insurance for myself and my wife. Even though my wife didn't have a paying job (although she did work harder at home than she ever did in the restaurant), if something happened to her, I would have to be able to pay for all the work she did, such as laundry, cooking, cleaning, and homeschooling. Looking back, I got a great deal and saved a ton of money by her staying home!

I was just at a Jake & Gino event, and a member named Daniel was there with his six-month-old baby. Daniel and his partner were invested in thousands of apartment units, and he has so many responsibilities to tend to on a daily basis. We were teaching asset protection and estate planning, and afterward, I asked him if he had established a guardian for the kids or even begun the process of writing a will. I loved the fact that he brought his baby to a real estate event, bouncing him comfortably in a snuggly.

But when he told me he had dropped the ball, in his words, it didn't surprise me. I sent an email to our attorney so he could start the process. If you feel like you don't have time for yourself, then *make* time for your spouse and your partners. Otherwise, you may be putting your partners at serious risk.

I learned that weekend exactly what could happen if you passed away without making a plan. One of our members told a story of a partner passing away while the partnership was in the midst of listing a property for sale. Unfortunately, the partner did not have proper estate planning, and his estate went into probate. It took over 18 months to straighten out, and it held up the sale of the property. By the time they finally sold, the market was in correction, and they lost millions of dollars.

A will is just the beginning. The next goal is to have your heirs avoid probate court, where they might wait weeks, months, or even years to get to stand in front of a judge trying to prove that they have a right to the property. To avoid this costly, very public courtroom scenario, let's take the next step of creating a living trust, a trust that goes into effect and protects you while you are alive and also lives on past your death. There are various ways to set them up, whether separately or jointly. You're going to be placing certain types of assets into this trust so that you and your trustees have joint control of these assets.

What type should you set up? (Not so) simple answer: "It depends." It depends upon your unique circumstances and your goals. What a living trust does is it puts into place your long-term wishes. While you're alive, you have complete control. But when you become incapacitated or die, it can be easily handed to the next generation.

Every living trust has three key roles:

1. **Grantor:** The person who creates the trust and puts their belongings into it.
2. **Trustee:** The person who controls the trust.

3. **Beneficiary:** The person who has the right to all of the benefits in the trust. While you're alive, that would be you.

When you are alive, you will be playing all three of these roles. You can add more stuff, and you can pay for anything because you are the beneficiary. When you pass away, your heirs avoid probate because the trust continues—only the names attached to the roles change. There's a new trustee and beneficiary named by you in the trust. Your assets can be passed on without any court or probate process.

You can also utilize a children's trust, which allows parents to leave assets to children while controlling the age at which they have access to them. There are some pretty cool provisions you can add in. If you don't want your 18-year-old to receive a windfall, you can have the inheritance spread out over the years. Once again, I selected 25, 30, and 35 years old as the ages when my children could receive their share.

You can install conditions, such as having a child attend rehab in order to receive benefits. There are also provisions you can add if there's a hardship or if a child wants to buy a home or open a business. Only *you* know your kids, so that's why the conversation is so important. You need to come up with a good reason why you'd want your kids tapping into their inheritance early. Starting a business, finishing college, or buying a home? YES! Buying a Lambo? Hard NO! (Unless there was a way for them to earn a cash flow from the Lambo.)

Another trust that can be very important to consider with families that have children with special needs is a special needs trust. If you have a child with special needs and want to create a trust for them in case something happens to you, call your estate attorney. There *are* some disadvantages, such as the cost and complexity of administering one. But there are also some important benefits, such as preserving eligibility for government benefits and protection against exploitation.

Now that we have our living trust set up, let's discuss our living will—your desires for what will happen to you in the case of an extreme medical condition. It's a legal document that tells the doctors how you want to be treated if you can't make your own decisions about emergency treatment. Sit down with your spouse and discuss what you want to happen if an emergency arises. Imagine the stress on your already panicked family if you leave the decision up to them in the moment!

I would also consider creating a durable power of attorney, which gives someone else legal authority to act on your behalf and continues in force even if you lose your mental capacity. My attorney explained it to me as "checkbook control." A durable power of attorney remains in effect even if you are incapacitated for any reason.

As you're going through your estate planning, I don't want you to confuse this with asset protection. I've heard some people say that because they've set up their living trust, they have protection from creditors. Not true. Protecting your assets from lawsuits is a whole other conversation, and a very important one if you want to protect your legacy from creditors.

My good friend Kraig Strom, who is an asset protection expert, often teaches our Jake & Gino community about asset protection. He is famous for saying, "Protect your assets from creditors, predators, floozies, and gigolos." In this country, over 40 million lawsuits are filed every year. You don't want to be vulnerable if one of those lawsuits is directed at you.

Kraig is also famous for saying, "It depends," when asked about types of entities to use or the structures that people should employ. At first, I just called that response "typical lawyer jargon." But, as I learned the differences in laws among the states, as well as different objectives that people are trying to accomplish with asset protection, I came to agree with Kraig. It depends. Listening to an asset protection strategy on TikTok is not where you should be getting your legal advice. It may be a good start, but follow it up by picking up the phone and contacting an asset protection attorney.

If you want to talk to Kraig's company, Barth Calderon, email me at gino@jakeandgino.com, and I'll connect you with them. They've done excellent work for my family and the Jake & Gino community.

Now that you're working on your estate plan and asset protection, the next step is a big one. I wish I could tell you I'd been doing this part for years, but I'd be lying. I realized that I had accumulated a ton of LLCs, bank accounts, mortgages, and insurance policies. Sorting all of this out would have been a nightmare for my family if something had happened to me.

Please take some time to start collecting all of your accounts and create a master document listing them all. I would put them all in a Google Doc. Also, write them on a piece of paper (or print out the Google Doc), and put the paper in your safe.

Start by itemizing your jewelry, art, and any other collectibles. Next, document your non-physical assets, such as your savings, checking, and stock accounts. Writing down all your entities would be next: LLCs, S Corps, and C Corps.

Your insurance policies would be next. Include your home, auto, disability, long-term care, and life insurance. According to Guardian Insurance, in the U.S., there's currently over one *billion* dollars in unclaimed payouts. Now would be a good time to review all the beneficiaries on your policies as well.

Then, turn your attention to any debt that you have: your mortgages, lines of credit, credit cards, and loans on vehicles. Whatever obligations you've incurred, let your family know what and where they are.

This next step may be a bit time-consuming, but it's just as important. Review the titles, deeds, and operating agreements on all your properties. This is something that I did with my attorneys to make sure my properties were deeded properly.

This seems like an exhaustive list, and I was initially overwhelmed just at the thought of it. To help you avoid feeling that way, I'm going to give you a checklist at the end of the chapter that will make it easier for you to take this one step at a time. The key is this: once you've finished it, the list needs to be reviewed at the minimum yearly. I've gotten into the habit of adding assets to the list immediately after buying them.

Up to now, we've focused on the financial aspect of legacy. When people join the Jake & Gino community, most of them join to attain financial freedom and leave a legacy to their families. I often hear the catchphrase "generational wealth," and I wholeheartedly agree about leaving the next generation in a better place. But I want to share with you *my* definition of generational wealth. To me, it encompasses not only money but values, traditions, life lessons, and skills.

You can look back in history at certain wealthy families, such as the Vanderbilts, who amassed enormous wealth but squandered it over the generations. Cornelius Vanderbilt left his family over 95 percent of his estate, with a value in today's dollars equaling over *$200 billion*. Not too shabby. His son William doubled the family fortune, but that was the end of the growth of the Vanderbilt estate.

The focus of William's heirs went from being producers to massive consumers as they built mansions all around the country and became wealthy socialites. Anderson Cooper, the CNN anchor, is a descendant of Cornelius. He has claimed that when his mother, Gloria Vanderbilt, passed away in 2019 at the age of 95, that was the end of the money as well; it never made it to his generation.

Remember our Baby Money Soldiers analogy from Chapter Four. It's not how many BMS you have; it's how you utilize them. The Vanderbilts slaughtered their BMS, and even more tragically, they left future generations unprepared to use their wealth responsibly.

In contrast, the Rockefeller family's results were quite the opposite. John Rockefeller's wealth was estimated to be around $300 billion when he passed away in 1937 (in today's dollars). His family was able to keep the fortune together, and John was credited with creating the first family office back in 1882. He was someone who understood how to expand and protect their BMS. In fact, the family is still worth over $8 billion, even with all of the philanthropic work that they're involved in.

Squandering the wealth doesn't bother me as much as creating entitled, useless heirs who have no appreciation of what they've been bestowed. They're not even grateful for what the previous generation sacrificed, built, and passed on to them. And whose fault is that?

I blame the generation that created the wealth. It's *their* duty to involve their family in the legacy component. What you don't want to happen is to build a real estate empire, leave it to kids who have no idea how to maintain it, and have them become motivated sellers because they had no idea how to manage the assets. Jake and I buy from these motivated sellers all the time.

Instead of only leaving your kids legacy wealth, consider leaving them legacy *skills*. My children will all be reading this book, along with all the other books my wife and I have written. They will also read the books on our book list. I'm teaching them how to invest in real estate and build a real estate business through the Jake & Gino community educational videos and by having them invest their hard-earned dollars alongside mine.

When I created the Jake & Gino platform, my sole purpose was to create another cash-flowing business. Little did I know that it would become one of the cornerstones of my financial legacy. Years from now, my grandkids will be watching me on YouTube and learning all about money and finance from me!

I often hear many wealthy people complain about their children and state that they're going to leave the majority of their assets to charity. I can understand why. They haven't prepared their children for the burden of becoming financial stewards. The irony is that most of us use our kids as an excuse for why we work so hard.

Well, I'm working so hard for my kids to provide for them and to create generational wealth. Have you ever asked your kids if they want you to work so hard? Maybe they just want you to spend a bit more time with them. While you're out there grinding, *always* involve your family in your money affairs. The goal is to create a Happy legacy, which will, in turn, create Happy money for the next generation.

Next steps to securing your Happy legacy:

1. Create a will
2. Form a living trust
3. Create a living will
4. Select guardians for your children
5. Consider a children's trust

These are the basic steps to begin your estate plan. If you already have a plan, be sure to review it with your attorney and update it accordingly.

Next, contact an attorney to discuss asset protection.

Then, start to itemize your assets and liabilities:

1. Itemize your personal inventory
   a. Jewelry
   b. Art
   c. Furniture
   d. Other collectibles
2. Document your non-physical assets
   a. Checking account
   b. Savings accounts
   c. Stocks
3. Review any life insurance policies and beneficiaries
4. List out all of the properties that you own

5. Itemize all the debt that you have
   a. Mortgages
   b. Car loans
   c. Lines of credit
   d. Credit cards
6. Review all of your deeds and operating agreements of your entities
7. Have guardians selected for your minor children
8. Consider creating a children's trust to disburse assets

As I'm sure you've heard before, a journey of 1,000 miles begins with a single step. The key is to pick a single item and start there! Whenever I think about not letting my family down, that's all the inspiration I need to get my legacy in order.

CHAPTER 9

THE HAPPINESS OF GIVING AND GIVING BACK

It's not how much we give but how much love we put into giving.
—Mother Teresa

It was my first Thanksgiving without my father. He had just passed away in August of that year, and my family was invited to St. Joseph's Friary in Harlem to help cook Thanksgiving for the Friars and the neighborhood. The Friars are brothers and priests who take vows of chastity, poverty, and obedience and follow in the footsteps of St. Francis. The communities that the Friars live in are impoverished, and many in the neighborhood come to the doorsteps of the Friars for food and company.

When I heard that we were preparing a meal for over 150 people, I thought to myself, "What did I sign up for?" I had never cooked more than one turkey at a time, let alone the ten turkeys they were planning. And Thanksgiving isn't complete without mashed potatoes, sweet potatoes, string beans, spiral ham, apple pie, pumpkin pie, and penne vodka. (It wasn't my idea to cook penne vodka. It was a request from some of the brothers who had visited our house.)

Despite all my dread, that Thanksgiving turned out to be a beautiful, transformational day for me and my family. I still felt sadness over the loss of my dad, but being invited into the Friars' community and sharing my talents with them brought me true happiness. They would have been appreciative if I had simply donated the food for the day. But spending the day together, preparing the meal, praying together, and serving the neighborhood is an experience that I'll never forget.

Most of the people we served that day had tough lives. They lived alone, struggled with some type of addiction, or had just fallen upon difficult times. I remember seeing the looks on their faces when my children were serving them, witnessing the joy that spread throughout that room, and hearing the laughter, all because we came together and served them. That feeling of community and service left an indelible mark on me, and I decided to return the following year. In fact, we continued the tradition until 2020, when COVID made it nearly impossible to gather together. But I'm going back this year!

Before this experience, I had always thought of charity as donating some money to an organization, such as United Way or Doctors without Borders. What I realized on that day was the connection that we made with the Friars and their community and the impact that it had on our family were far more precious than a simple donation. We spent time speaking with our neighbors and getting to know them. There was one woman named Carol who loved my lentil soup and Italian cheesecake. Every year we went, I would bring down her own bowl of soup and cake to bring home, and she would have gifts for my kids.

Throughout this process, my children realized how fortunate we were, how many things we took for granted, how many people in life had serious challenges, and how spending time with someone could radically change their lives. It was a reminder to us not to take life for granted and to be thankful for everything we have, especially our happy family.

I felt the love in that room that day, and it wasn't from the food. The Friars' dedication and commitment to the neighborhood embodies the quote from Mother Teresa at the start of the chapter. They have very little to give in terms of money, but they put so much love into giving. That's what I want you to consider when picking a charity or donating your time.

When I was younger, I was convinced that the size of my donation mattered most, but I've come to believe that the love and intention far outweigh the money. That was good news for me! At the time, I didn't have a lot of money to donate, but I did have a lot of love and a few talents.

Where can you start if you want to become more charitable? If you're a good cook, how about donating your time to a food kitchen or assisted living facility? You love sports? Consider coaching Little League baseball or giving tennis lessons to someone who can't afford to pay. Do you love to sing? Start a choir or donate your time to teach people.

Thomas Fuller eloquently stated, "Charity begins in the home, but should not end there." Early on in my marriage, I was fixated on my personal situation and how I was going to take care of my family. I can honestly say that I was consumed by the scarcity mindset, but something happened to me that Thanksgiving Day at the Friary. I felt the love and the joy that comes from giving to others. It was such an uplifting experience to be able to bring joy to others and to start living a life of gratitude. That's what I think charity can do for your life.

Charity does lead to happy money, but it needs to start in the house with you being the child's role model and involving them in the decision-making process. I can't imagine not involving my children on that day with the Friars. Your kids need to be part of the experience.

I remember my father being very charitable to his friends and family. Whenever we would go to Italy, he would have one suitcase filled with presents for all of his relatives. Back then, things were much cheaper in the U.S., and you couldn't find many of these items there. I can easily recall how happy it made him feel to be able to share with his extended family.

This is where happy money can have a huge impact on your life. I've had so many blessings over the years from welcoming the Friars into my home. I was using my money in happy ways to help the Friars along with the neighborhood they served. That money sure was bringing joy to the community.

Now, I'm a huge Yankees fan, and in the last chapter, I shared with you George Steinbrenner's quote on charity: "I don't care about the money. I care about the legacy." To say that Steinbrenner was abrasive is a massive understatement. He fired his manager Billy Martin five times, he was notorious for his rants to his players, and everyone referred to him as The Boss.

But there was another side of Mr. Steinbrenner that most people did not witness: his unwavering commitment to charity. His charitable acts often flew under the radar, and he stipulated that no one would know who gave the donation, so it wouldn't attract attention. That concept has pretty much disappeared in this day and age. George embodied the true spirit of charity, that of being able to share something with someone with the expectation of nothing in return.

That's where I think you'll receive the most joy—when you donate your time or money without waiting for accolades to pour in. It's such a wonderful feeling to be able to help someone yet not expect anything in return. The irony of life is that your charitable event won't go unnoticed. You'll see benefits popping up in your life elsewhere.

I think that the experience had such a profound effect on my children that they grew stronger in their faith and decided to incorporate it into their lives. My oldest daughter, Gabriella, became a full-time missionary with an organization called LifeTeen after she graduated college. Her initial job was to host retreats for summer campers, and then she joined their travel team to go to parishes across the country and work with those who couldn't afford to come to their camps.

My son is currently working for LifeTeen this summer on the facilities team, taking care of the grounds and helping with daily camp activities. I was completely surprised and proud when they both decided to volunteer and serve others. They're living their core values of faith and charity, and the experience has only strengthened their faith.

My hope is that my children will ultimately become leaders, and I think the only way to become a better leader is to be able to serve others first.

One book that's impacted the way that I approach business and life is *The Go-Giver* by Bob Burg. We had the privilege of interviewing Bob twice on the Jake & Gino show, and his insights and teaching of adopting a go-giver attitude contradict conventional wisdom.

Joe, the protagonist of the story, is a hard-charging, make-it-happen kind of person, but he's stuck in a rut. He's trying to land a key sale at the end of the quarter and goes to seek advice from a consultant named Pindar. Pindar teaches Joe about the Five Laws of Stratospheric Success. At first, Joe is skeptical of what Pindar shares with him, but he ultimately learns to shift his focus from getting to giving, putting others' interests ahead of his own, and always looking to add value to their lives.

People sometimes confuse donating money to charity as solely being a go-giver, a person who's able to take the focus off their needs and add value to the lives of others. In the book, Bob takes it one step further and expands upon the definition. To him, it means to be a giving person, someone who gives their thought, their attention, their focus, their time, and their energy to others. In short, it's one who gives value to another.

I'd like to share the fourth and fifth laws from the book as they relate to charity. The fourth law, the Law of Authenticity, is sharing the gift of yourself. This law is about being open to sharing your time and energy with others without expecting to get anything in return. The way to be authentic in life is to choose things that align with your values. If you can authentically give of yourself, people will connect with you on a deeper level.

Authenticity is a challenging one for me, especially being a father. It can be difficult to show your kids when you fail, you make a mistake, or you don't know the answer. However, your kids will respect you and love you even more if you show up as your authentic self.

The fifth law, the Law of Reciprocity, is a challenging one for most of us. The key to effective giving is to stay open to receiving. When someone would thank me or pay me a compliment, I would deny it or say, "It's no big deal." Now, I thank them and let them know how important it was for them to take the time to share their kind words with me. I have allowed myself to be open to receiving thanks, and I, in turn, continue to give more of myself.

How do you want to define your legacy? You have the opportunity to create a legacy of charity and hope if you decide today to start focusing on or continue to focus on helping others and creating value in other people's lives.

Next steps to creating a charitable legacy:

- Remember times in your life when the charitable actions of others have made a difference.
- Think about the causes that matter to you most.
- Decide how you can use your skills to help.
- Involve your family in your acts of charity, especially your children.

THE HAPPY LEGACY JOURNEY

Congratulations on taking a huge step toward your happy money, family, and legacy. I want to thank you for taking the time to read about these three very important aspects of our lives and learning how to optimize them for *your* life. It all starts with you being the leader and casting the vision for what your family looks like, both today and for generations into the future.

The first step is to define what happy money means for you. Happy money will make it much easier for you to create a happy family, and you can share your money beliefs with your kids. It will also allow you, as a family, to start planning and building a happy legacy.

This is a journey that never ends. In fact, while I was writing this chapter, I took a walk with my 18-year-old daughter, Sofia. I love her with every fiber of my being, and my wish, and hers, is that she marries a wonderful man and is able to be a stay-at-home mother and raise her kids. She's witnessed firsthand the impact her mom has had on her and her siblings and wants to have the same connection with her own children.

As we were walking, I talked to her about the trusts that I've created and how I would like to be able to pass on wealth to her and her siblings. I said, "What if I could give you a stipend every month to pay for monthly necessities, which will allow you to stay at home and not have to work to pay the bills?"

I quickly followed that up by saying that if that money was being spent on jewelry or vacations, then it would cease to flow. Sofia was in total agreement with the stipulations that I laid out to her.

These individual conversations are important because each child will likely have different opinions. Some of them may want to open their own business or buy an apartment complex.

Even with all the wealth I've created, I don't want to spoil my kids, but I do want to help them when I'm gone. You hear so many stories of wealthy people leaving all of their money to charity, to their pets, or to some other cause because they were estranged from their children.

I hope that one of the main things you're getting from this book and these ideas is to avoid having spoiled, entitled kids. You want to create responsible stewards for your wealth for the next generation who will pass along your values and your legacy. And how great would it be if I could start sharing my wealth with my kids and grandkids while I was still alive? Talk about happy money!

The **first step** I suggest taking as a family, if you haven't already, is to create a family budget. I love to show my kids how much things cost and make them understand why we buy certain items and pass on others. I want them to create healthy spending and saving habits, and the key is to show them, not constantly tell them that you can't afford it or that money doesn't grow on trees. I would rather tell them that the vacation to Italy isn't in our budget this year because I'm saving for college, and that braces and contacts are really expensive. I want them to learn and to realize they can direct their Baby Money Soldiers wherever they choose to, but that some choices are wiser than others.

The best course of action with your family is to be honest with them about your finances. If you decide to hide your struggles, they'll still sense something is wrong, and you'll lose an opportunity to teach them how to work through hard times. It's said that when we allow ourselves to be vulnerable to others, we open the door to greater connection and a deeper relationship. When I decided to ask for forgiveness from my children and show vulnerability, our relationships *did* grow deeper.

Next, I want you to try to avoid one of the biggest mistakes I committed when teaching the kids about money. If you've enjoyed reading this book, you're probably going to find it hard to resist the temptation. *Please*, do not force the conversation of money and finance on your children at too early an age. Your kids have their own unique personalities. Some will naturally gravitate to the conversation, while others will find it as painful as getting a tooth pulled.

Take it slow. You'll be shocked by how much they learn just by watching you, and when they're ready, they'll come up with a bunch of questions. Start by playing games and give them easy books to read. The key is to make learning fun and entertaining.

My daughter Sofia made me realize just how much kids absorb by watching you. Early on, I was overbearing with her and forced her to read my books as well as some of Dave Ramsey's. When I came to realize that doing so was counterproductive, I pulled back and let her come to me when it was in her self-interest. Once she graduated from massage school and became a therapist, boy, was she ready with questions:

"How do I take payments from clients? What type of accounts should I open at the bank? Should I create an LLC? How much should I charge? What about a website? How do I get more clients?"

It was awesome! I was there to guide her and to get her set up. And, if you recall, we have monthly meetings with our bookkeeper to make sure everything is on track. If I had pushed her too hard when she was younger, though, I don't think she would have come to me for help.

Finally, think about ways your family can be more philanthropic. What is it that excites your family, and who do you want to create an impact for? I wish for you not only to create streams of income but also streams of *purpose*. Money isn't your reason; it only funds it. I want you to think of how you can give back now and in the future in ways that are meaningful to you.

I want to sincerely thank you for taking this journey with me on how to create Happy Money, a Happy Family, and a Happy Legacy.

To learn more on how to work with me, visit
https://jakeandgino.mykajabi.com/ginobarbaro

BOOK LIST

Our Books

1. *Wheelbarrow Profits®*
2. *Honey Bee*
3. *Baby Money Soldiers®*
4. *Family, Food & the Friars*
5. *Multifamily Real Estate Booklet*
6. *Creative Cash*
7. *The Cannolis Exploded*
8. *A Gelato Blast*
9. *Pizza with a Purpose*

Books mentioned in *Happy Money*

1. *Rich Dad Poor Dad* by Robert Kiyosaki
2. *Mindset* by Carol Dweck
3. *The 7 Habits of Highly Effective People* by Steven Covey
4. *Dr. Orman's Life Changing Anger Cure* by Dr. Mort Orman
5. *Happy Money* by Ken Honda
6. *The Psychology of Money* by Morgan Housel
7. *Secrets of the Millionaire Mind* by T. Harv Eker

8. *The Five Love Languages* by Dr. Gary Chapman
9. *The Go-Giver* by Bob Burg
10. *Know Can Do* by Ken Blanchard
11. *Think & Grow Rich* by Napoleon Hill
12. *Atomic Habits* by James Clear
13. *What Would The Rockefellers Do?* by Garrett Gunderson
14. *Limitless* by Jim Kwik

Additional Recommended Reading

1. *Richest Man in Babylon* by George S. Clason
2. *Never Split the Difference* by Chris Voss
3. *Cash Flow Quadrant* by Robert Kiyosaki
4. *How to Win Friends and Influence People* by Dale Carnegie
5. *The War of Art* by Steven Pressfield
6. *Killing Sacred Cows* by Garrett Gunderson
7. *The Alchemist* by Paulo Coelho
8. *The One Thing* by Jay Papasan

ABOUT THE AUTHOR

Gino Barbaro is an investor, business owner, educator, entrepreneur, and podcast host. As an entrepreneur, he has grown his real estate portfolio to over 2,200 multifamily units transacted and $400 million in assets under management.

Gino and his business partner, Jake, are teaching others how to do the same through Jake & Gino, the premier multifamily real estate education community. Their students have closed over 80,000 units and have $5 billion in deal volume!

He resides with his beautiful wife, Julia, and their six children in St. Augustine, Florida.

To learn more about Gino, visit
https://jakeandgino.com/link-tree/
https://www.barbaro360.com

www.ingramcontent.com/pod-product-compliance
Lightning Source LLC
Chambersburg PA
CBHW020407130626
46549CB00006B/2465